Vietnam
Combat Commander

Vietnam Combat Commander
A Memoir of Two Tours

COLONEL (RET.) GEORGE R. MAULDIN

Foreword by ROBERT C. JOHNSON

McFarland & Company, Inc., Publishers
Jefferson, North Carolina

Unless otherwise noted, all photographs are from the author's collection. Portions of this work have previously appeared in George R. Mauldin, *Your Sons—My Soldiers—Our War: A Vietnam Commander's Struggles* (AuthorHouse, 2005).

ISBN (print) 978-1-4766-9908-0
ISBN (ebook) 978-1-4766-5798-1

LIBRARY OF CONGRESS CATALOGING DATA ARE AVAILABLE

Library of Congress Control Number 2025041943

© 2025 Colonel (Ret) George R. Mauldin. All rights reserved

No part of this book may be reproduced or transmitted in any form or by any means, electronic or mechanical, including photocopying or recording, or by any information storage and retrieval system, without permission in writing from the publisher.

Front cover image: Captain George Mauldin holding a Viet Cong flag captured by one of the platoons during a big cordon operation, February 1969; *background* © Shutterstock.

Printed in the United States of America

*McFarland & Company, Inc., Publishers
Box 611, Jefferson, North Carolina 28640
www.mcfarlandpub.com*

I dedicate this memoir to the men and women
who served in the Vietnam War in any capacity.
A special recognition to the fighting men
who risked so much and, in some cases, lost so much.
Above all, I dedicate this memoir to the memory of
Sergeant Santana S. Fernandez, Jr., aka Mouse,
who sustained mortal wounds while
aiding a wounded fellow soldier.
Last, this dedication must include the men who served
in Company C, Sixth Battalion, 31st Infantry
under my command.

Acknowledgments

Superlatives have not been found to express my appreciation for the professional and timely support I received from Susan Kilby of McFarland. A mound of gratitude to one of my best subordinate officers in Vietnam, Michael Strand, for recognizing potential in my work and steering me to McFarland. I am grateful for the collaboration of fellow veterans in general and Gary Stoltz in particular. My gratitude to Robert C. Johnson for applying his masterful skills and literary genius to the foreword. A huge shout-out to my grandson Tyler Mauldin for his support with graphics and website creation. I received enviable support and encouragement from my writing group, the Writer's Roundtable, of Dover, Tennessee. Last but not least, my wife Kathy deserves an abundance of accolades for lending her sharp eye to the editing and proofing process.

Table of Contents

Acknowledgments   vi
Foreword by Robert C. Johnson   1
Preface   5

Part 1—Bizarre Things That Happen in a War Zone

    I. All Creatures Big and Small   11
    II. Angry Centipede   16
    III. Landing Zone Robin   23
    IV. Monkey See, Monkey Do   27
    V. Snakes Galore   32
    VI. Once Upon a Claxton Fruitcake   36
    VII. A New Life   41
    VIII. The Saigon Girl   49

Part 2—When Things Go Wrong in Combat

    IX. Landing Zone Wool   57
    X. The Orangutan Caper   64
    XI. Kicked Out Two Stories Up   69
    XII. A Lot of Bull   74
    XIII. The Unsent Letter   77
    XIV. Rushing Waters   82
    XV. Careless Enemy   86
    XVI. The Enemy Celebrates   93

Table of Contents

XVII.	Fateful Night Mission	100
XVIII.	The Reluctant POW	110
XIX.	Duck Boy	119
XX.	The Rebellious Soldier	125
XXI.	When Superiors Make Mistakes	130
XXII.	Stealth Mission	136
XXIII.	Left Behind	149
XXIV.	The Old Man's Kill	156
XXV.	A Soldier Called Mouse	162
XXVI.	A Different Mission	174

Military History: Colonel (Ret.) George R. Mauldin   183

Index   187

Foreword
by Robert C. Johnson

    I first met Colonel (Ret) George Mauldin in a coffee shop in the small northwestern Tennessee town of Paris more than a decade ago. I overheard him talking to someone about a fact-gathering mission to Somalia he had been on back in the 1980s when he was a specialist in Middle Eastern affairs for the U.S. Army. In this capacity, George had learned to speak fluent Arabic and Hebrew and had served in several postings to the region, including Saudi Arabia, Israel, and Oman. I insinuated myself into that conversation, and from the beginning I felt a tremendous rapport with and respect for George. We shared a lot of the same interests in history, both political and military, and compatible views on contemporary politics and culture.

    George and I could not have been more different in many respects. I was what you might call an ivory tower "intellectual" with a doctorate in German literature. George was a career officer in the army with two combat tours in Vietnam as a career infantry officer and was awarded a Silver Star for valor. In addition, I am more the indoor type while George is a lifelong hunter and fisherman, who, to this day, a man in his early eighties, gets up well before sunrise on cold autumn and winter mornings to hike into the woods to kill and dress a deer. I have never known a stronger or more self-reliant individual. I feel deeply honored that he asked me to write a foreword for his memoir about his experiences in the Vietnam War.

    George joined the army as an enlisted man in 1960 and served in an artillery unit in Germany. In the coming years, he graduated from Officer Candidate School and was commissioned in the infantry in the rank of second lieutenant. As part of his initial training, he completed airborne school and served in multiple airborne

Foreword by Robert C. Johnson

assignments, including a tour with the storied 82nd Airborne Division. The army sent him to serve his first tour in Vietnam, where he arrived in early January 1966, when he was just 24 years old. He was assigned to a company in the Eighth Cavalry, First Air Cavalry in the Central Highlands, where he was platoon leader for a mortar platoon and executive officer of his company. Upon completion of this tour, George served stateside for a couple of years before returning to Vietnam in the fall of 1968. This time, George, now a captain, was assigned to be commander of Charlie Company, Sixth Battalion, 31st Infantry, 9th Infantry Division, operating in the Mekong Delta.

I have read many histories of wars, campaigns, and operations. I have read numerous fictional accounts of war. Nowhere have I read anything that so effectively conveys the daily reality of war as George's memoir. The vignettes contained herein carry the reader from the routine, pedestrian functioning of army bureaucracy through the farcical workings of chance to the abrupt terror of sudden, violent death and injury and the ensuing sense of loss and grief. From the process of collecting and distributing payroll to the troops to a urine-soaked aerial odyssey with Michelle the monkey to the heartbreaking deaths of Duck Boy and Mouse. From hilarity to tears. From enjoying steak and a cold beer at the divisional base camp to cautiously making way through a treacherous landscape filled with booby traps. These pages give an authentic sense of the daily operations of a rifle company in Vietnam.

In a sense, George's memoir could be seen as something of a handbook for young infantry officers. He describes the deliberations, the discussions with superiors and subordinates that lead him to the decisions he makes. Of course, random chance, the unknown, and, above all, the enemy always have a say. In this honest, understated account, we see men functioning under enormous strain and doing the very best they can under the circumstances. Indeed, Goerge and the men fighting under his command exhibit that quality of courage that Ernest Hemingway so admired, "grace under pressure."

With the deepest respect for those men and others like them who have fought, suffered, and died at the bidding of their country, I highly recommend this fine memoir to the reader.

Robert C. Johnson studied for a year as a Fulbright Scholar at the University of Munich and holds a doctorate in German language and literature from the

Foreword by Robert C. Johnson

University of Washington. He has an undergraduate degree in history and has maintained a great interest in political and military history throughout his life. Dr. Johnson is a retired university administrator and real estate investor. He resides in the town of his birth, Paris, Tennessee.

Preface

This book was prompted by my experiences in South Vietnam during two one-year tours. The first tour was January–December 1966 when I served in the First Cavalry Division in the Central Highlands, and the second was October 1968–July 1969 when I served in the Ninth Infantry Division about 60 miles south of Saigon in what is labeled the Mekong Delta. Events are presented in two major categories: "When Things Go Wrong in Combat" and "Bizarre Things That Happen in a War Zone." When planning a combat operation, considerable effort goes into making certain that the mission is clear to all concerned and that due consideration is given to the effects of the environment and weather. However, when the enemy's unpredictable response is combined with a hostile environment, it is virtually inevitable that they will interfere with the best-laid plans. Adding to the fertile subject matter for my eager pen were the bizarre things that occurred, some of which were humorous and others tragic.

My objective in assembling such a collection of stories was to use this format to explain and highlight the many things that can happen to the fighting soldier. This war had several unique features, some of which are addressed. A prominent one was the nature of the threat to us fighting men. First, it was difficult at times to identify the enemy. The guerrilla, who was referred to as the Viet Cong (VC), was very good at his craft and had an uncanny ability to blend with the population. Then there was the 360-degree threat to us at all times. We fighting men were rarely able to rest on the notion that everything on one side of a line was friendly and everything on the other side was hostile. The only line, if it is to be called that, was the demilitarized zone (DMZ) between North and South Vietnam. I never served near the DMZ, only in the Central Highlands and the Mekong Delta.

Preface

The war's duration, when combined with the inadequate justification for the war by the government, resulted in disapproval by the general public and sharp criticism of the military. Such rejection and condemnation by our fellow citizens were heavy psychological burdens for me and other commanders of fighting men who were following our orders at grave risk of serious injury or death. My stories endeavor to show how these brave men fulfilled their enlistment oaths despite their many reasons to hide behind the skirts of a foreign flag in order to evade the draft.

These stories come from the heart and are true to the best of my recollection. In writing about my experiences, I drew on my own notes and collaboration with Vietnam veterans with whom I served. I also wrote some of the stories soon after returning from Vietnam the second time to ensure that I did not forget important details. I have used pseudonyms to protect the identities of people discussed.

Map of Vietnam, pre–Communist era (courtesy Tyler Mauldin).

PART 1

BIZARRE THINGS THAT HAPPEN IN A WAR ZONE

I

All Creatures Big and Small

My first trip to South Vietnam began in early 1966. I was a young lieutenant assigned as an 81 mm mortar platoon leader in the First Cavalry Division (Airmobile). I had been in the war zone about a month when my platoon got its first night ambush mission. We were to ambush a big trail that was a bit more than two kilometers from the division security perimeter. It was a common practice to order such small unit ambushes because they had proven to be especially effective at night when the North Vietnamese Army (NVA) or the VC guerrillas preferred to move people and supplies along the major trails and waterways of the Central Highlands.

My platoon members and I spent the last hour before darkness checking our weapons, radios, rations, and water supply. We also ate a quick C-ration meal before departing the company area. The first few hundred meters of travel went smoothly because it was not completely dark. My point man was following a compass reading of 185 degrees and my pacing man was keeping count of the steps. We were forced to travel in single file because it was far too dangerous to walk on established trails. Local guerrillas booby-trapped the trails with both explosives and punji pits and stakes. The going became much slower and difficult after full darkness set in because my point man was forced to cut his way through some of the thick vegetation with a machete.

My first squad was leading the way with 11 men. The squad leader was a mature and seasoned noncommissioned officer (NCO) whose judgment and skills I trusted. I followed with my radio operator and platoon sergeant. The remainder of the 20-man ambush patrol followed behind us.

We were traveling with as much stealth as possible given the fact that we were forced to cut our way through much of the vegetation.

Part 1—Bizarre Things That Happen in a War Zone

We were on radio silence except for the requirement to report to our company commander every hour on the hour. Several of us carried flashlights that were rigged with red lenses to prevent detection. With few exceptions, verbal exchanges were minimized or were whispered. Careless units had been ambushed in the past while traveling to an ambush site, and we could ill afford the risk of such a possibility.

When we were within about 500 meters of our objective, every man in the lead squad stopped abruptly. Obviously, that dictated that we all must halt and wait for the signal to move again. Nobody moved. I waited patiently for the squad leader to either move or come and tell me why we were stalled. Within a few seconds, he made his way through the brush, breathing fast, and speaking excitedly.

As soon as the sergeant caught his breath, he began to speak. "My point man stopped suddenly and walked back to me, sir. He was as white as a ghost. He said that there's something big slightly off of the route that we're taking. He says he can hear it breathing and it sounds big and might hurt somebody if we don't back up and go around it. Also, if it's one of the larger animals from this region, like an elephant or a water buffalo, it could kill or injure several of us before we could kill it."

I was anxious to get to our ambush site because the optimum time to catch the enemy on these trails was between 2200 hours and 0200 hours. To take a circuitous route would significantly delay our arrival at our destination. I was apprehensive about approaching the source of the sounds, but my curiosity was too strong to turn back.

"Come on, Sergeant Williams. Let's see if we can identify this monster."

I followed the squad leader back to the front of the squad where we found the frightened point man. I asked him to tell me what the excitement was about.

"Well, sir, it sounds like some animal inhaling and exhaling slowly. It's hard to determine its exact location. It almost seems to move as it breathes, yet I've heard no sounds of footsteps. You don't suppose it's a big snake, do you? I've never heard anything like it. I'm hesitant to guess at what it might be because there are just too many possibilities. Seems like everything in this land wants to sting you, bite you, or eat you."

"OK, if we've angered a king cobra, we must be extremely

I. All Creatures Big and Small

careful. He can move fast, and in the darkness, we can't tell where he's traveling. Sergeant Williams, tell everyone to stay back while you and I move closer and use our lights to spot this creature."

After the sergeant issued his instructions, he and I moved forward, following the point man a safe distance from the ominous sounds. As we approached, I heard the whooshing sound that began relatively quietly and ended in a crescendo. Every hair on my body stood at the rigid position of attention. I imagined that all creatures known to me could be standing in the darkness waiting to pounce. I thought of tigers, elephants, water buffalo bulls, and venomous snakes. I asked the other two men with me to remain still so that I could hear the sound better. The breathing pattern made it appear omnipresent. Stranger yet was the way in which the sound began relatively weak and ended each time in a crescendo. My curiosity would not permit me to turn away. I simply had to determine the source of such unusual sound.

I advanced cautiously in the direction of the sound and shined my military-issue flashlight at waist level in the direction of the presumed creature. Seeing nothing that could account for this bizarre sound, I removed the red lens from the light and again shined it in the direction of the sound, expecting to see eyes reflected by the light source. Unable to identify any creature, I cautiously walked a few steps closer, shining the light on the ground ahead of me and as high as chest level. As I drew closer to the unidentified source, it became clear that my footsteps instigated the sound, which prompted me to focus on the ground. I had images of a hooded king cobra weaving his head to and fro. After stamping my foot deliberately on the dried leaves, the whoosh sounded ahead of me a few feet. I focused the light beam on the ground and soon discovered the source of the sound.

Some of the smallest of God's jungle creatures had traumatized half a platoon of big, brave soldiers for nearly a half hour. It was a colony of termites. They had abandoned their old mound and were traveling overland under the protection of darkness to another site.

I was truly relieved to discover that it was creatures at the bottom of the food chain rather than an apex predator. Fortunately, I remembered a great deal about termites from my high school biology class and could have explained right away why these bizarre creatures emitted such a strange sound when they were on the move. At the time, however, I was anxious to proceed, so I only stated that it

Part 1—Bizarre Things That Happen in a War Zone

Second Lieutenant George Mauldin. This photograph was taken the morning after the ambush patrol in which we were frightened by the colony of termites. When the photograph was taken, I was recovering and cleaning my M-16 rifle. The entire Second Battalion, Eighth Cavalry had the duty of securing the First Cavalry Division perimeter, and my company was assigned a sector. Note that I am wearing standard army fatigues instead of jungle fatigues and leather jump boots, which were not yet available for issue. The leather boots presented many podiatric problems because they did not drain well, and the smooth leather soles resulted in unstable footing in the wet jungle. January 1966.

I. All Creatures Big and Small

was termites and that they posed no threat to us. I urged my subordinates to move with haste to our ambush site so that we could fulfill our mission. If the enemy used that trail that night, he did not travel through our well-prepared kill zone. I know because I was awake and alert the entire time. At sunrise, we began our trek back to the First Cavalry Division base camp.

The next day, after we had returned to our company area and were able to catch a few hours' sleep, I explained to the members of the platoon that only the king and queen termites, plus most of the reproductive types, have eyes; however, they have very poor vision. All of the workers and soldiers are blind, and they constitute the majority of the termites in any colony. A blind worker leads the colony when it is on the move, and when he contacts an obstacle or threat, he emits a clicking sound. As this warning is repeated, it travels through the remainder of the colony, building to a virtual crescendo as it reaches the termites in the rear. Hearing this ominous sound caused our imaginations to contribute in no small measure to the fear factor. This is the way of the jungle.

I learned during my two combat tours in South Vietnam that the jungle always holds another surprise for the unsuspecting.

II

Angry Centipede

It was early spring 1966 in the Central Highlands of South Vietnam. Subordinate elements, along with the battalion headquarters of the Second Battalion, Eighth Cavalry, air assaulted into the jungle several miles north of the city of Pleiku. We expected enemy contact because First Cavalry Division intelligence had reported radio transmissions from a major NVA unit in that vicinity.

I was platoon leader of the battalion heavy mortar platoon, which was usually co-located with the battalion forward command post on such operations. The 81 mm mortar platoon provided general fire support to the battalion's subordinate units during operations, and the mortar crewmen nearly always augmented the security perimeter around the battalion command post. The heavy weapons platoon, which was assigned to the same company as the mortars, frequently augmented the security around the battalion command post as well.

We were airlifted into this landing zone (LZ) by UH-1 Huey helicopters, which could transport as many as six combat-loaded American troops in each aircraft. With their single-turbine engines, these choppers, when loaded, required significant running room in order to acquire what the pilots labeled "lift." This running room was vital when they were loaded and were required to clear any obstacles such as a 110-foot jungle canopy.

Our arrival at the LZ went without incident—no sign of the enemy. My platoon sergeant immediately began placing security on our perimeter and dispatched two men on a listening post about 50 meters into the jungle. The mortar crews began immediately to set up the mortars and prepare them for action. I went to the commander of the 105 mm artillery battery, which had been airlifted to the LZ by larger, more capable helicopters known as Chinooks. The

II. Angry Centipede

artillery battery was also required to augment the security around the battalion command post, so I coordinated a linkup of forces to ensure that there were no gaps in our perimeter.

After coordinating with the artillery battery commander, I went by the battalion command post to notify the battalion operations officer that our security was in place and to receive any special instructions. While waiting to speak to the major, I overheard the aviation company commander explaining an issue that constituted a significant problem.

He explained that the choppers had no difficulty in delivering the troops to this particular LZ and that they likewise had no difficulty in lifting off from the LZ while empty. There was a problem for the helicopters, however, in exiting the LZ when loaded because they would be unable to achieve lift in time to clear the jungle canopy. He urged the battalion commander to request engineer support to clear a significant number of trees and stumps to give the choppers more room for liftoff.

I exited the tent soon thereafter and returned to my platoon to check the readiness of the mortars to execute their mission. After the mortars were fully prepared to conduct fire missions, everyone began digging. The mortar crews dug emplacements called parapets, and everyone else, including me, began digging foxholes. The men on the security perimeter dug foxholes which also served as fighting positions. We had been busy with our intense defensive preparations for more than an hour when we heard the unmistakable blades of a CH-47 Chinook helicopter beating the air. After landing in the LZ, it discharged about 25 engineers with chainsaws and other supplies and equipment. Soon after the Chinook lifted off, we heard another helicopter's blades, but the sound made in this case was most unusual.

When it came into view, I immediately labeled it a Flying Mosquito. Slung underneath its belly was a small bulldozer. The pilot cautiously and tediously brought the giant helicopter into the middle of the LZ. The blades continued beating the air as ground crewmen disconnected the bulldozer. When the green hunk of steel was disconnected, the large helicopter lifted only a few feet from the ground and began moving within the tree-bordered confines of the LZ instead of flying away. The pilot maneuvered it several yards and hovered over a UH-1 Huey that had remained behind when the other

Part 1—Bizarre Things That Happen in a War Zone

A CH-54 helicopter (commonly referred to as a Flying Mosquito) lifting off after delivering a small bulldozer, which was used by the engineers to clear the landing zone. Early spring 1966.

II. Angry Centipede

lift ships flew away. After moving directly over the smaller chopper, men began lashing the UH-1 to the belly of the giant. Soon afterward, the large chopper lifted the UH-1 off the ground and held it in a static position presumably to check load distribution. Then it demonstrated its immense power by raising its cargo vertically from the LZ sufficiently to clear the jungle canopy.

The sound made by the "flying crane," as it was called, was growing faint when we heard one of the engineers shout, "Fire in the hole." We all scooted for cover because that is the universal warning that an explosive charge is about to be ignited. KABOOM! A deafening blast felled several large trees at the western boundary of the LZ and sent large chunks of wood in all directions. After several more blasts, the bulldozer began clearing trees and debris in an effort to lengthen the LZ. When the engineers finished their work at sunset and made themselves available to augment security during the night, that concluded the excitement—so I thought.

I quickly dug a shallow hole and placed a heating tablet in it in preparation for heating some C-rations. After cutting a green branch from a tree and cutting two short lengths to place over the hole, I opened a can of ham and lima beans, added some hot sauce, and placed it over the heat source. I lit the heating tablet and waited to see the steam rise from the beans. When my food was hot, I opened some C-ration crackers and ate my meal. After consuming my meal, I heated some water in my canteen cup and mixed some C-ration cocoa with the hot water. After satiating my hunger, I brushed my teeth.

During the initial operations briefing by my company commander, he emphasized the threat of malaria in this particular area and reminded us of his policy regarding prevention. At dusk, we were required to apply insect repellent to all exposed skin, roll down shirt sleeves, and button the top button of our shirts. Those of us who were in relatively static positions brought jungle hammocks. When suspended between two trees, they were comfortable and their side nets prevented insects from gaining entry.

I set up my hammock near the mortars and my radio operator. I then spread my poncho on the ground near one of the large trees to which my hammock was tied. I removed my jungle fatigue shirt and applied insect repellent over my entire upper torso, arms, hands, face, and neck. I slipped my shirt on and sat down so that I could lean

Part 1—Bizarre Things That Happen in a War Zone

against the tree. I did not plan to slip into the hammock until at least midnight because my platoon sergeant and I would check our part of the security perimeter at least twice before the midnight hour.

I sat leaning against the tree listening to the commands that were given by the men who computed the firing data for the single mortar that was firing harassment and interdiction rounds off into the jungle. The mortars and the 105 mm artillery guns fired such rounds onto specified targets—for example, major trail junctions and major waterway junctions as well as other locations from which radio transmissions had been received. I was also thinking about the following morning when I would be on tap to lead a patrol around the area to ensure that there was no enemy activity.

Suddenly, I felt a very sharp pain on the left side of my lower back just above my beltline. I knew immediately that it was a bite and that it was imperative that I identify the source. I knew that if it was a snake, it had to be venomous because nonvenomous snakes do not have fangs to deliver such a painful bite. I jumped up and ran to my pack to retrieve my flashlight. I removed the red lens, turned it on, and began looking all around my poncho to find the culprit. I didn't see anything until I lifted a corner of the poncho near where I had been seated. There on the ground, staring back at me, was a centipede between nine and 10 inches long. It was the largest and most ferocious-looking centipede I had ever seen. It scurried deeper under my poncho, so I just let it stay hidden because I wanted to capture it alive. I yelled out to one of my sergeants near the mortar that was firing to bring one of the empty cannisters in which we transported mortar rounds. I also yelled for my radio operator to come over and help me catch the centipede. Catching it became much easier than expected. After opening the cannister and slipping it beneath the poncho liner near the centipede, it quickly crawled into the cannister, and my radio operator quickly trapped the critter.

I called my platoon medic and explained what had bit me. He was curious to see its size, so I handed him the cannister and said, "For God's sake, don't let it escape. It deserves to die a slow death. The explosives that were set off by the engineers must have uprooted it and caused it to exact its revenge on me."

By this point in our tour of duty, we all knew that centipedes were venomous, but no one, not even my medic, could speak authoritatively of the effects of this bite. He demurred and suggested that

II. Angry Centipede

I seek advice from the senior medic who traditionally accompanied the battalion headquarters on such operations.

As I walked the approximately 50 meters to the battalion command post, I could feel the venom tingling under the skin on my left side as it spread upward toward my armpit. When I finally located the senior medic, his first order of business was to examine the bite marks. Upon seeing them, he confirmed that fangs had penetrated the skin. Then he asked to see the centipede. I handed him the cannister and cautioned him not to permit the creature to escape.

After seeing the critter, he proclaimed, "That's the biggest one of these I've seen. I've heard of large jungle centipedes like this, but I've never seen one. You may be in for a rough time for 24 to 48 hours. You'll probably have a headache and some trouble controlling muscles. Also, you may have trouble tracking objects with your eyes for this period of time. I have an antihistamine injection that I can give you, which will help to slow the spread of the venom in your body."

After my consent to proceed with the shot, I followed him into a small tent adjacent to the command center, and he asked me to remove my shirt. In his examination, which included eye movement, he asked me to raise my left arm. He probed around the fang marks and pressed gently on the glands under my arm. He suddenly asked if I always had a knot under my left armpit. I told him no and immediately felt under my arm to find a knot nearly the size of a ping-pong ball.

He administered the shot and handed me some pills for the headache, and upon leaving the tent, the difficulty with eye movement predicted by the medic became apparent. I noticed that I was having difficulty holding my eyes steady. As I lifted the flap to exit the tent, he said, "I wouldn't try to go on any trips into the jungle for at least twenty-four hours. You won't be able to stay out of trouble with your eyes bouncing around like I see already."

I had a miserable night because of the headache and twitching muscles. I did not move around much either because of the effect the venom had on my eyes. In fact, my platoon sergeant checked the men on the perimeter without me.

The next day, the bright sunlight hurt my eyes and I still could not focus well, so one of my trusted junior sergeants took the patrol around the area in my stead. By the morning of the third day, the effects of the venom had subsided so that my vision was near normal.

Part 1—Bizarre Things That Happen in a War Zone

We were under orders to prepare for an air assault on a different target, so it was time to pack up the mortars and our personal gear. Our policy was to leave nothing that could benefit the enemy, so we started a fire in one of the foxholes where we burned C-ration boxes and cannisters from which we had taken 81 mm mortar rounds. It was finally time to roast the centipede. I moved the cannister that held it captive slowly toward the fire. I wanted it to feel the intense heat in increments—to panic and want to escape. I left the cannister near the fire until it began to smolder; then I removed it and opened the lid. I had succeeded in roasting the critter and exacting my revenge, so I threw the cannister into the burning coals, thinking that I had seen and felt the last of this vicious jungle creature.

Beginning later in 1966, I became aware of a knot forming under the skin at the site of the venomous bite. It grew over the years to the size of a ping-pong ball. Apparently, my body had responded to the bite by trapping some of the venom and sealing it in the shape of a sphere. I was aware of the small sphere under my skin but did not think much about it until it began to cause me pain in 1996. I complained about it several times to a number of doctors, but when I explained the probable cause of the knot, they downplayed its importance and suggested that I ignore it. I continued to complain about the knot periodically because it pained me more frequently. Eventually, a surgeon at Bach Army Community Hospital, Fort Campbell, Kentucky, agreed to remove it. After removal, I was permitted to examine the specimen, which was a benign, spherical, white mass that had in fact grown bigger than a ping-pong ball. Finally, after 33 years, I was rid of the angry centipede. Maybe the removal of the last vestiges of the painful bite cheated the jungle creature out of the last word.

III

Landing Zone Robin

In early March 1966, I was the leader of an 81 mm mortar platoon in the Second Battalion, Eighth Cavalry, First Air Cavalry Division (Airmobile). The company-size unit to which my platoon belonged had been operating out of the Bong Son region of the Central Highlands of South Vietnam for several weeks. We were notified early one morning that the entire battalion would be airlifted to a new area in response to a hot intelligence tip.

We packed our equipment for the airlift to the new area as usual. The three rifle companies of the battalion were picked up by choppers first and inserted into the new LZ. The company to which I was assigned was inserted last, along with the battalion forward command post (CP). As usual, members of my mortar platoon and the heavy weapons platoon were expected to augment the security for the battalion CP. The reconnaissance platoon, which belonged to the same company, was usually dispatched to scout the area and report enemy activity.

When we finally arrived at the new LZ, I made my usual assessment and observations. The LZ was flat and covered with rich, green grass, similar in appearance to a pasture for cattle. It was surrounded by thick forest, with the moisture content heavy on all the vegetation. The ground was also wet and felt soft and saturated. I noticed a small stream a few meters inside the wood line.

Without any prompting from me, my platoon sergeant selected four sites for mortar emplacements, and the men began digging immediately. Soon after our arrival, the much larger CH-47 helicopters began arriving with 105 mm howitzers and sling loads of artillery ammunition swinging beneath them. The howitzers and ammunition were lowered to the ground within 100 meters of our location.

Part 1—Bizarre Things That Happen in a War Zone

Within a few minutes, I received a radio call from my company commander instructing me to come to his location. Upon arriving, he informed me that the recon platoon had been dispatched on its mission and that I was to take a few of my men and conduct a quick recon on the far side of the stream. I took my radio operator and five more men and struck out in the direction of the wooded area.

The stream was small, roughly the equivalent of a shallow creek. We waded across and spread out with at least 10 meters between each man. My radio operator and I took a well-worn trail and had not traveled far into the area before discovering a series of abandoned jungle huts, which we called hooches. Each one was built on stilts elevating it at least four feet off the ground. We were to discover soon the reason for the elevated living quarters.

My first surprise was the number of hooches and the evident expertise in constructing and camouflaging them so that they fit perfectly within the jungle canopy, making them virtually undetectable from above. It was evident that this particular enemy unit had been in this location for a long time and that families must have been present.

As we walked slowly and cautiously through the area, I was focused on the trail, looking for trip wires or other indicators of booby traps or mines. Suddenly I noticed a long black object stretched across the trail. Thinking it was possibly a snake, I called my radio operator forward to see the mysterious creature. The critter was not convincing as a snake because it did not appear to have scales, so I touched it with the tip of my rifle. Water squirted from it, resulting in contraction like a typical earthworm. It was indeed an earthworm whose body was at least the diameter of a quarter. At about one foot long, it was the biggest worm I had ever seen.

The next surprise came when the sergeant and the four troops with him came closer and asked, "Have you seen these yellow-and-black worms? They're on the vegetation and seem to want to climb on us. I've had three on me already."

I told him no, that I had not noticed them and didn't know what they were or why they wanted to climb on us. We were soon to discover that these brightly colored miniature vampires were leeches—and they were aggressive. They were on the vegetation and on the ground. Their favorite tactic appeared to be crawling onto tall grasses and low-growing brush and falling onto hapless victims.

III. Landing Zone Robin

Not long after seeing the huge earthworm, some of the men spooked a number of wild chickens. I had never seen chickens that could fly like them. They were small and lean and could fly with the agility of a wild bird. My next surprise was most pleasant.

A couple of my men yelled that they had spotted several young pigs. After some discussion, I was convinced that they were perfect eating size, so I contacted my company commander by radio and asked permission to kill a few and cook them over an open pit. He first notified the battalion forward CP that there would be some rifle shots coming from our direction; then he gave me permission to take some pigs. The men killed five that were roughly 40–50 pounds each. Several men who had grown up on farms were in my platoon. They knew what to do with wild game and, within a few minutes, had field dressed all five pigs. We cut young saplings and tied two pigs per pole to transport them to the LZ. After returning to our company area, we shared three of the pigs with the artillery unit.

Some of us began digging mandatory foxholes while others skinned the remaining two pigs. Later, they cut them into halves so that they could be attached to our makeshift spits. Since it was too dangerous to have open flames after dark, we dug a separate foxhole and kept a fire in it the remainder of the day to ensure an adequate source of heat all night to cook the pigs.

By the next morning, the pigs were cooked, so we treated ourselves to a fresh barbecue breakfast. Since the men routinely carried ketchup, hot sauce, and garlic, which they received in care packages from home, we even had barbecue sauce. One of them combined the ingredients and made a passable sauce. We did not eat all of the delicious pork in one meal. As a result, we were able to carry the remainder in our backpacks for a couple of days and enjoy our pork meals multiple times.

We determined later that the brightly colored leeches were called tiger leeches by the Vietnamese. For me, they were terrorizing. Most leeches live in the water, so a victim must be in the water for one of them to attach itself. These miniature monsters, however, could climb anyplace—and they did. A man in my platoon woke one morning with a one-and-a-half-inch vampire worm attached to his eyelid. The critter had embedded his bloodsucking appendage in the corner of the victim's eyelid, requiring evacuation to the rear for treatment. In fact, my platoon medic administered a morphine

Part 1—Bizarre Things That Happen in a War Zone

shot to the young soldier because he was having panic attacks. He kept screaming that he was afraid of losing his eye. I slept very little all three nights that we were in LZ Robin. The threat from the black-and-yellow miniature vampires fueled my phobia at night to the point that I sat on my steel helmet rather than lie on the ground. When exhaustion eventually overcame my fear, I laid on the ground. Predictably, the next morning several of the critters were attached to me. To this day, I get goose bumps when remembering the variety of leeches that are found in South Vietnam and the many times that they feasted on us.

IV

Monkey See, Monkey Do

In late 1966, I was executive officer of a company-size unit of the Second Battalion, Eighth Cavalry, First Cavalry Division. Our battalion's mission was to be part of a blocking force near the South China Sea coast to prevent elements of the NVA from escaping our cordon by sea. During one of our numerous night ambushes, the recon platoon killed a number of VC guerrillas, and one of them had a small monkey tied to his waist with a rope.

Although frightened by the firearms and explosives, the monkey was unharmed. It was obvious that the monkey was habituated to humans. The small animal was wary of us and hesitant to tolerate all of our differences from its previous owner. It accepted the shorter men among us more freely than the taller ones. We were fascinated by the small animal and decided to take it with us to the company CP as we returned from the ambush. We initially thought the monkey to be a male and one of the troops suggested the name Michael. A short while later, someone stated that the critter was actually a female, so we changed the name to Michelle.

Well, Michelle was the subject of a lot of attention. We shared our C-rations with her, and that was generally her sole source of food until one of our platoons purchased some bananas from local Vietnamese. We were located several miles north of a forward support base named LZ English. Our unit supply sergeant operated from LZ English, and when possible, he would send some warm breakfast items by helicopter to the company. One morning, he sent boiled eggs, doughnuts, and a large thermos of coffee. The reaction from the troops would have made you think that it was a high-dollar spread in a five-star hotel.

None of our units ever took the monkey on operations, although she could have been an excellent source for early warning. Monkeys

Part 1—Bizarre Things That Happen in a War Zone

have keen hearing and vision, both of which are superior to most humans. Her care and feeding fell to me and our operations sergeant. One of our sergeants was a native of Guam and seemed to know a great deal about jungle animals. Based on his suggestion, I gave Michelle one of the boiled eggs. She took it, examined and smelled it, and placed it on the ground near her as if she did not know what to do with it.

I naively reached and picked it up. That was not a wise decision, for she lunged at me and caught my right leg in her front paws. Before I could back away beyond the length of her rope, she bit me inside my thigh and screamed at me. I don't speak monkey, but I could understand that she had just called me a low-life thief and declared as only a monkey can that I deserved the bite. I tossed the egg toward her and she caught it. This time, she smashed the egg against a nearby tree and began eating it.

The end of September was fast approaching, which meant that in my capacity as executive officer, I must return to the First Cavalry Division base camp at An Khe to pick up the end-of-month pay for the unit. I knew that a supply helicopter was inbound to our location, so I was preparing to catch a ride back to LZ English. As I was collecting my gear and M-16 rifle, my company commander informed me that I should take Michelle with me. In his words, "She will be much better off in the rear where she will have proper shelter and better food." By this point in time, Michelle was accustomed to me and permitted me to pick her up and carry her to the helicopter.

As we approached the helicopter, its engine was running and the large main rotor was turning. Michelle clung tightly to me as I walked under the turning rotor and boarded the helicopter. Her eyes were wide and she was turning right and left as she faced me and clung tightly to my jungle fatigue shirt.

That was basically the situation until the helicopter began to lift off the ground. She could see that we were much farther from the ground than she had ever been, and she pulled so hard on my shirt that it tore on both sides near the top pockets. Concurrent with hearing my shirt ripping, I felt the flow of warm urine in my lap. She must have emptied her bladder, for she wet the entire front of my jungle fatigue pants. She clung tightly to me for the duration of the 20-minute flight to LZ English.

We had to wait nearly an hour in LZ English for a helicopter ride

IV. Monkey See, Monkey Do

to the city of Qui Nhon, which was a principal U.S. military sea port and logistics base. From Qui Nhon, I planned to catch a flight on any plane that was headed for the First Cavalry Division base camp in An Khe. During the chopper ride to Qui Nhon, Michelle clung so hard to me that her grip left blood blisters on my skin, and she urinated on me again. We waited in the U.S. Air Force passenger terminal for about two hours before catching a C-130 flight that was bound for the First Cavalry Division base camp.

The flight by C-130 was fast, but it was traumatic for Michelle. This particular aircraft is famous for being extremely noisy. The fact that Michelle could not see out of the plane seemed to contribute to her fears. After the plane gained sufficient speed to lift off from the runway and the crew threw the switch to lift and store the landing gear, the poor monkey panicked like never before. The loud screeching sounds of the hydraulic pumps caused her to grab my fatigue shirt with all four paws, force her head into my shirt, and urinate on me again. Needless to say, I was happy to arrive in An Khe. My pants were still wet and I was beginning to smell. Poor Michelle was pretty agitated too. After landing, I used the field phone in the small terminal to call the company supply sergeant and ask him to pick us up and drive us back to the company area.

Michelle was an instant hit with the troops in the rear area. I had a jungle sleeping bag and cot in the officers' quarters and she "slept with me" for two nights while the supply sergeant located a cage and longer leash. Neither of us got much sleep those first two nights because she insisted on sleeping either on my sleeping bag or cuddled next to it. That was OK except she was not housebroken. She would urinate on me, so I eventually tied her where she could not reach my cot. That did not work well either because she would whine to return to my cot where she could sleep next to my warm sleeping bag. By the third night, the supply sergeant had procured a cage big enough for her. We decided to position the cage in the company orderly room where either the first sergeant or the company clerk was present much of the time.

I spent two additional days in the division base camp as I waited to pick up the pay from division finance. I spent much of that time during daylight hours in the orderly room discussing supply, pay, and personnel issues with the unit clerk. We took Michelle from the cage early each morning, fed her, and placed her on a leash. Most of the

Part 1—Bizarre Things That Happen in a War Zone

unit personnel, who were in the "rear area" for a variety of reasons, usually visited the orderly room at some point during the day. They were naturally fascinated with Michelle and her story. It became clear that we had to post a warning sign near her area and on her cage because if given something—that is, food of any kind—she was very possessive of it. Likewise, if she was not necessarily given something but considered it her property, she behaved the same toward it. A couple of the troops discovered her intense possessiveness the hard way because they were bitten and scolded in monkey language

A young soldier dropped in one morning after Michelle had been treated to a banana, some grapes, and half an apple. He walked near where she was tethered on her leash and picked up the banana to move it closer to her. She leaped and grabbed his arm, snatched the banana from his hand, bit him, and screamed at him as only a monkey can. Soon, we all became acquainted with her jungle manners and tolerated her habits and quirks.

She habitually became energized in late afternoons and, if free from her leash to roam, would find her way to the rafters in the open ceiling. These rafters were spaced three feet apart, and she would frequently demonstrate her amazing strength and agility by traveling very fast from one end of the room to the other by jumping from one rafter to another.

One of the times when she was free from the leash, we discovered that she liked beer and mimicked humans when she drank too much alcohol. Several of us were sitting around in the orderly room sharing war stories late one afternoon with a couple of new troops while Michelle was allowed to run about free of her leash. Suddenly, one of the new troops called our attention to Michelle, who had picked up his beer can and was drinking from it. I thought she would taste it, dislike it, and toss it aside. Surprisingly, she continued to drink until she finished it. When questioned, the young soldier said he thought that there was only a small amount remaining in the can.

Within five minutes after drinking the beer, Michelle began to act silly and bold. It was clear that she was unsteady when she walked, but we did not comprehend to what degree her coordination had been affected until she climbed up to the rafters and attempted once more to demonstrate her trapeze skills. Her first leap from one rafter to the next met with disaster. Instead of catching the rafter as usual, her front paws missed it completely, and she hit the rafter

IV. Monkey See, Monkey Do

with her nose and fell to the floor. The company clerk and I jumped up at the same time and ran toward her. He reached her before I did, picked her up, and placed her in her cage. It was evident that Michelle was drunk and was JWI (jumping while intoxicated).

We made the decision at that time that we must guard our beer cans and not leave them sitting around. Michelle clearly could not hold her liquor. I departed South Vietnam in December of that year, and when I left, Michelle was doing well and still entertaining the troops with her creative antics.

V

Snakes Galore

In the late summer of 1966, I was the executive officer of a company-size unit of the First Cavalry Division which was deployed in a blocking position on the South China Sea coast. Our mission was to prevent the enemy soldiers of the NVA from escaping our encirclement by way of the sea. The NVA soldiers were clever at escaping to the fishing villages along the coast and confiscating fishing boats that belonged to civilian fishermen. The NVA soldiers, who were trapped within our encirclement, were desperate to escape and had made numerous attempts to sneak through our lines over the past several days and nights. They made most of their breakout attempts during hours of darkness.

Unique to this operation was the direct support that was provided by the U.S. Navy. Boats that were called "swift boats" patrolled the sea coast day and night and were in direct contact with our unit by radio. These boats were captained by enlisted men of chief petty officer rank and were manned by a crew of five. They were armed with an 81 mm mortar in front and .50 caliber machine guns front and rear. They were also equipped with passive night vision sights and radar, which gave them great visibility over the water without the use of lights.

We appreciated knowing that the swift boats were patrolling and could be called on to support us should that become necessary. This was a unique arrangement for us infantry troops, so my commander and I had become accustomed to communicating with them several times a day as a routine matter but also had called on them to check some suspicious boats on several occasions. The skipper told us in one of our conversations that he and his crew patrolled a stretch of the coast about 50 miles long, so they were not always near our location. These boats were over 51 feet long and were powered by

V. Snakes Galore

twin diesel engines that could propel them to speeds in excess of 35 miles per hour.

Late one afternoon, the skipper of the swift boat that patrolled the waters near us contacted us by radio. It seemed that he and his crew were returning from the city of Qui Nhon, which was 40–50 miles to the south, where they had refueled and replenished their food supplies. He then asked if the company commander and I would like to join him and his crew that evening for cold beer and steak. We could hardly believe our ears. We looked at each other and asked, "Did he really say cold beer and steak?" We immediately answered with a big "hell yes." The skipper asked if we were still in the same location as two days prior, and we confirmed that we were. He then said that they should reach us by late afternoon. He added that they would anchor within 30–40 yards of the shore and that we should look for a way to reach the boat without getting soaked with salt water.

We decided to use two inflatable air mattresses. I had one in my pack and one of the enlisted men lent us another one. By the time the boat pulled up near shore, it was nearly sunset. After stripping to our underwear, we tied our jungle fatigues and boots in a bundle and laid on the inflated mattresses on our backs. With the bundles on our abdomens, we used our hands to paddle to the boat. When we reached it, a couple of crewmen took our clothes and shoes and helped us aboard. Our feet were wet from dangling off the ends of the mattresses, and my underwear was damp in the rear where I had splashed water while rowing.

As soon as we were dressed, we were served a cold Budweiser. We limited our beer consumption to only one each because we had good reason to expect a possible engagement with desperate enemy fighters during the night. While we consumed the beer and discussed operations, one of the crew grilled the steaks. He then served the steaks on real plates with metal utensils. Making the situation more surreal was finding two leaves of fresh lettuce with two slices of tomato and a thick slice of Vidalia onion stacked on the plates. To drink with the meal, we were served a cold Coca-Cola in a can. For us, such a meal was fit for royalty. My commander and I had a fleeting feeling of guilt, knowing that the troops in the company were eating C-rations and washing them down with warm water. By the time we finished the meal and made small talk about hometowns, the sun had settled over the horizon and darkness had invaded the scene.

Part 1—Bizarre Things That Happen in a War Zone

The crewman assigned to stand watch for most of our visit suddenly called out to the skipper, "Chief, you've gotta see this. I've never seen them so active."

The chief pushed away from the small folding table, excused himself, and walked to the fantail. He looked over the side and exclaimed, "Captain, you and your XO [executive officer] need to see this."

We walked to the aft section and looked over into the water. My fear and dread were betrayed by the feeling that my eyes were as large as ping-pong balls. The water was alive with long black-and-white sea snakes. I guessed that some of them had to be over six feet long. My commanding officer spoke before I did but left no doubt that he was equally concerned about the swim that we had to make from the swift boat to the shore. He turned to the chief petty officer and asked, "Are they always this active?"

The chief stated, "No, they're not usually this active—it's their mating season."

The challenge we faced in keeping our bodies and clothes dry while committing no act that would offend the venomous snakes was daunting. When I finally settled onto my inflated mattress, my entire thought process was overshadowed by my fear of the snakes. There was simply no escaping them if you were in the water. The dread that they might actually swim onto my air mattress was ever present. I did not want any part of my body touching the water that was not essential to returning to shore. While paddling to the boat, I had let my feet hang in the water. However, when I mounted the mattress to return to shore, I pulled my feet onto it. This act committed more of my body weight to the air mattress and pretty well soaked my lower body, but I didn't mind. I bade farewell to the skipper and his crew and paddled toward shore as fast as I could with only my index and middle fingers on each hand dipping into the water. The panicky return to shore splashed water on my jungle fatigues, soaking my clothing with salt water. I rationalized and justified my fear and dread with the fact that at least I was not bitten by one of the most venomous snakes in the world.

I will end this story by repeating some of the things I concluded about South Vietnam while serving in some of its worst places. It's a place of small people and small warm-blooded animals. Most other critters are large. In the places where I spent much of my time,

V. Snakes Galore

the environment could cause your demise if you were reckless and careless. Many of the jungle critters could bite you, sting you, eat you, or just plain kill you. Thus, the word to the wise is, "Expect the unexpected."

VI

Once Upon a Claxton Fruitcake

It was late November 1966 and I was assigned as the XO of a company in the First Cavalry Division in South Vietnam. The company had been deployed for several weeks in the Pleiku/Kontum area of the Central Highlands. When my duties as XO permitted, I stayed full time in the jungle with the company on operations. I had left my unit in the jungle recently and flown by helicopter to the division base camp near the Vietnamese village of An Khe. My purpose in returning to the rear area was to collect the unit's pay from the division finance and fulfill my duties as unit paymaster. I planned to return to the jungle immediately upon signing for the pay and deliver payment in military payment certificates (MPCs) to every available member of the unit, including my company commander.

It was my first day back in the rear area and it was nearing time for mail call, so I made my way to the company orderly room where the mail clerk would arrive soon with the mail. Mail call in a war zone is one of those occurrences that excites soldiers—it's a hallelujah moment, especially if you receive some mail. I was very excited when the unit mail clerk called my name and handed me not only a couple of letters but also a small package. I was in disbelief when I saw my father's name in the return address block of the box. He was a loving father, but he wrote few letters and had never sent a package to me. Besides, I had written to him recently, reminding him that I had completed nearly 11 months of my 12-month tour and would be coming home in December in time for Christmas.

I took possession of my booty and sought refuge in the small circular tent that I shared with my company commander. I had a flash of indecision about whether to open the letters or the package first;

VI. Once Upon a Claxton Fruitcake

however, my ambivalence gave way quickly to overpowering curiosity about the contents of the package. When I removed the protective packaging from the inside, I was totally thrilled. It was Claxton fruitcake, consisting of four rectangular sticks—each one wrapped individually in cellophane. I simply couldn't wait to sample the cake.

I pulled my survival knife from its sheath and cut a generous piece from one of the sticks. I placed it on my tongue and slowly closed my teeth on the moist sweetness of the delectable treat that surely was divined by Gabriel. I was not a fan of store-bought fruitcakes, but this was extraordinarily delicious. The various fruits in it tasted genuine to say the least, and it was moist. I ate several more slices before I could restrain myself. I decided to take one whole stick with me to share with my commander when I returned to the jungle.

As the two senior officers in the company, my company commander and I shared a small, circular tent. The company supply sergeant had found enough plywood to construct crude wall lockers for us. We were able to hang our uniforms in them and organize other clothing and shoes on the three shelves. There was one shallow shelf at the very top where I kept my service cap for my dress green uniform. After eating my fill of the cake, I placed the remainder on this shelf for safekeeping. The wall lockers came with hasps and locks which provided limited security.

The next morning, I drew a .45 caliber pistol from the company armorer, went to division finance, and signed for the hundreds of dollars in equivalent MPCs. Afterward, I returned to our company area and packed my gear, which included a whole stick of the fruitcake. I left the remainder of the fruitcake on the top shelf of my wall locker and secured the double doors with a lock. I was then driven by jeep to the division airfield, where I signed up for space on the next available aircraft that was destined for LZ English. From that LZ, I could catch a helicopter lift to my unit in the jungle.

I reached my unit two days later and immediately began paying available troops. I realized that there would be a delay in paying the men of the reconnaissance platoon because they had not returned from a long-term recon mission. It would be another two days before the recon platoon would return, and as I expected, my stay in the jungle was extended. In the meantime, the soft-sided briefcase was my constant companion because it still contained a large sum of

Part 1—Bizarre Things That Happen in a War Zone

MPCs. Over the course of my stay in the jungle, my company commander, the operations sergeant, and I finished the stick of fruitcake that I'd brought with me. In conversation with my commander, I mentioned several times that I had two whole sticks plus about a third of another in the unit area and how I was anxious to return and devour the remainder.

Finally, on the fifth day, I paid all the remaining men available and was ready to return to the division base camp and unburden myself of the residual currency. I caught a helicopter ride from the jungle to LZ English, then a lift on a fixed-wing aircraft called a Caribou to the 1st Cavalry Division base camp. After arriving at the division airfield, I called the company first sergeant and asked him to send a jeep to transport me to division finance. The company clerk arrived shortly and drove me to division finance where I was required to account for all funds. This process was time-consuming because I was one of several paymasters returning funds on that day.

At last, the company clerk dropped me off at the circular tent where I had left the remainder of my fruitcake. I was quite happy with the idea that I would sleep on an army cot again for several nights instead of in a poncho and liner on the ground. That is, I was happy until I slipped under the front flap of the tent and saw the condition of my wall locker.

Both doors were open wide. I noticed immediately that my Petri camera, which was stored inside the wall locker, was missing. That was a big disappointment, for I had an unfinished roll of 35 mm film in the camera that had photos of a fellow officer who had been killed in enemy action only recently. However, another disappointment was yet to come. When my eyes moved to the top shelf, I discovered that at least half of one of the sticks of fruitcake that I had left behind was missing. My instincts caused me to assume that the dirty rotten thief who broke into my wall locker had helped himself to some of my fruitcake. As I moved my gaze from the fruitcake, I thought I saw movement behind my service cap. I slid it slightly to one side, and there appeared the culprit. A creature with a pointed nose, whiskers, beady black eyes, and a file tail was staring at me from behind my service cap.

It was a large rat with a distended belly. I think it was still licking its lips from its most recent meal of my fruitcake. I started talking to it.

VI. Once Upon a Claxton Fruitcake

"You're going to die, big boy. Your fruitcake heist calls for the death sentence. I won't let you get away with this egregious violation. I want to shoot your sorry ass, but I know I can't because division policy makes it a court-martial offense to discharge a firearm unless there is enemy action. I will cut your damned liver out, though."

A dartboard hung outside one of the wall locker doors with darts sticking in it. I began throwing darts at the rat as he shifted from one side of my cap to the other to avoid the sharp objects. Finally, his fear was such that he lunged forward and jumped from the top shelf of the wall locker. He hit the dirt floor running at full speed, escaping under the side of the tent where he had worn a trail as he entered and exited on his previous heists. While running outside to chase him, I pulled my survival knife from its sheath. The rat ran for the small stream that was a few yards behind our tent. I followed in hot pursuit. The stream was only about six or eight feet across and maybe a foot deep. He hit the water with a splash and began swimming upstream under the water. He was an impressive swimmer. After swimming several yards, he turned toward the bank opposite me to escape. Permitting him to escape was simply not an option, so I jumped the stream and blocked his exit from the water. He turned and swam downstream with me following along the stream's edge, again swimming underwater. He tried again to exit the stream, but I was waiting with my knife at the ready. He turned upstream again and swam a few yards and turned toward the bank opposite me to exit. This time, it was different, for I could see that he was exhausted. I watched as the thieving rat slowly dragged his fat body out of the water. I began talking to him again.

"It's time for you to meet your maker. I'm going to cut your liver out and maybe see the missing half of my fruitcake again."

After stabbing the knife completely through the rat, I took him back toward the tent and found a small bush where I tied him upside down so I could finish the surgical removal of his liver. Yes, there was sufficient evidence to show that he had gorged himself recently on fruitcake.

I left him hanging on the small bush near our tent so that other would-be thieves might see what their fate could be if they offended the owner of the Claxton fruitcake.

I spent at least two hours that night writing a letter to my father

Part 1—Bizarre Things That Happen in a War Zone

in which I thanked him for the cake and wrote the full story of the fate of the thieving rat. He never forgot the story and mentioned it in conversation many times after I returned to the United States, accusing me of "going overboard in punishing the rat."

VII

A New Life

It was early January 1969, and I was the commander of an infantry company in the Ninth Infantry Division whose area of operations was in the Mekong Delta region—about 60 miles south of Saigon.

My company had been conducting air mobile operations most of the day. I was ordered on our last insertion to sweep through an area of known VC activity. Then my entire company was to ambush a major intersection of two canals overnight. Late in the day, I moved the company within one kilometer of the ambush site and instructed the subordinate units to rest and feel free to heat and eat some C-rations.

At twilight, I ordered the company to begin movement to our ambush site. My thinking was that darkness would overcome us before we reached our destination, thus denying the enemy any opportunity to spot our exact location. We had never conducted operations in this area, so I was uncertain about what to expect. When we approached within about 400 meters of the canal intersection, my lead platoon notified me that there was an abandoned hooch near our trail. I instructed him to do a quick check to ensure that it was not inhabited and that I would have the mortar platoon conduct a detailed inspection upon our arrival to ensure that it was not booby-trapped.

I placed the first and second platoons on the larger canal and the third platoon on the smaller canal, and the mortar platoon was tasked to secure the rear. By the time I received confirmation from my platoons that everyone was settled in place, the sounds of crickets signaled the arrival of the night. I set up my CP in a cluster of trees several meters from the hooch. We rarely set up inside an abandoned hooch because it could contain a number of things that were harmful. A big threat was snakes that were attracted to rats that usually made their home in or near such structures.

Part 1—Bizarre Things That Happen in a War Zone

As soon as my platoons reported that they were in place, I carefully made my rounds to learn exactly where they were set up and make sure that they were arrayed in a safe pattern. I had barely returned to my CP when I heard the voice of my mortar platoon sergeant on the company radio net.

"Charlie Six, this is Charlie Four Bravo, over."

My radio telephone operator (RTO) on the company net handed me the receiver as I turned to face him.

"Roger, this is Charlie Six, over."

"This is Charlie Four Bravo. My elements just brought two Vietnamese women to me. They are both carrying loads with traditional sticks across their shoulders. One of them appears to be pregnant. They both keep chattering and pointing as if they wish to proceed through our area and reach the smaller canal. What should I do with them? Over."

I was aghast. I could feel my heart thumping in my chest. My near-panic mindset was only mildly relieved by the realization that these two women had walked into one of my platoon locations during the hours of darkness without being shot.

"From what direction did they come, and do you know if they used the waterway at any point? Also, do you have any reason to suspect that they were accompanied by anyone? Lastly, bring them to my location, but only after you've thoroughly checked the contents of their bundles. Over."

"This is Charlie Four Bravo. They came from the same direction that we did. They were on the trail that parallels the large canal. My men say that they were alone—just the two of them. We've already searched their bundles. They contain rice, some small fish, canned goods, some tea, and fresh vegetables. Over."

"Roger. Escort them to my location as soon as you can."

While waiting for the two women to show, I thought about the situation and its ramifications.

Should I have my men escort them through our lines, or should I force them to remain with us until morning? There are consequences for either course of action—some predictable and others totally unpredictable. If I let them pass through our lines, they might inform the local VC of our location, thus giving the enemy the opportunity to ambush us during the night or early in the morning. If someone comes searching for these women, it could easily result in us shooting them or

VII. A New Life

shooting each other. The possibility that causes me the greatest angst is that their family members or friends might come looking for them. If anyone approaches our perimeter from any direction during the night, his probability of being shot is very high.

I turned to my radio operator who was on the company net and asked him to tell the first platoon to send the tiger scout named Duc to my CP. Duc was one of the former VC guerrillas who had abandoned the Communist movement and signed an oath of loyalty with the Government of South Vietnam. Some of these men, like Duc, volunteered to serve with American forces as scouts. He spoke rudimentary English and could be useful in dealing with locals. As Duc was approaching my CP, I heard the sound of footsteps coming from the direction of the mortar platoon.

The mortar platoon sergeant led the small group with the two women following directly behind him and two men trailing, carrying the bundles that belonged to the women. The women appeared typical for residents of the remote villages. The pregnant woman was younger—probably in her mid-30s but looking much older. I guessed the older woman's age at 40, but she also looked much older. Her lips and gums were stained with brown betel nut, signaling that she had decaying teeth that likely caused her pain. They were both dressed in what we Americans called black pajamas, and they wore sandals. As soon as they spotted Duc, they began talking very fast and pointing toward the junction of the canals.

Duc listened for a couple of minutes, then turned to me and began to translate. "Woman say she afraid she have baby soon. She want to go home where old woman know everything about babies. She say she feel pain now from baby. I think, Captain, she will have baby quick."

I looked at Duc in silence as I thought about his words. "Duc, tell her not to worry. We have a doctor. My senior medic is very capable and can help her if needed. Tell her that I'm sorry, but they must remain here. It's too dangerous for them to move around after dark."

Duc turned immediately and began talking to the women. When I turned to ask my radio operator to call for my senior medic, he stepped from behind me.

"I've been listening, sir, and I'm confident that I can help. I'll take them inside the hooch and prepare a soft place with my poncho liner as a bed. I delivered two babies in Guatemala when I was on a mission for my church. I'll need some extra water from the canteens of two other men. I'll also need another flashlight and someone to hold it for me as needed. With your permission, Captain, I'll dig a hole in the floor of the hooch so that I can heat some water in my steel pot with C-4. I usually carry a couple of small towels for my personal use, so I'll use them as needed—if she actually has the baby."

"Sure. I'll donate half a canteen of water now and ask both RTOs to do the same. That should be enough with what you have. I'll also ask the RTOs to hang their poncho liners on the sides of the hooch to prevent the light from escaping."

Without any prompting from me, Duc led the way into the hooch with the two women following. The pregnant woman entered holding her abdomen and wincing with pain. I was convinced that she would have the baby soon.

I turned my attention to Staff Sergeant McCleod, who was the acting platoon leader of the mortar platoon. As commander of the company, I rarely had enough lieutenants to place one in the mortar platoon. I stepped away from my CP group, made eye contact with Staff Sergeant McCleod, and motioned for him to follow me.

Once we were a comfortable distance away from others, I turned to the sergeant and spoke. "Sergeant McCleod, I'm very disturbed at learning that these two women walked into your perimeter after dark. On the one hand, I'm relieved that your men didn't shoot and kill them. I'm confident that they are simple villagers making their way home. On the other hand, I expect to hear a good explanation from you as to why they could walk into your perimeter unchallenged. If they had been enemy soldiers, I could be requesting a medevac to evacuate wounded or dead soldiers from this unit. That is simply not the way I want things to go in my unit," I stated as I looked directly into the sergeant's eyes.

"Sir, I have good reasons but no excuses that would make either of us feel better about this situation. My men were focused on setting up the mortar in case it was needed. I emphasized to them that that was the priority. Consequently, they had not completed the establishment of the full perimeter. As they explained the situation to me, the two women walked in the well-used trail. The men swore that they never heard them until they were in their midst. They also explained that their black pajamas make it hard to spot them in the dark. I'm sure you realize, sir, that I'm short six men what with the

VII. A New Life

three men who were wounded by that big booby trap four days ago. We can and will do better in the future. I promise."

"OK. Let's defer any further conversation about this subject until we are back in a rear area. I have already asked the first sergeant to forward an urgent request for more men. By the way, I'm very concerned that family members or friends of these women may come looking for them, especially near daylight. Every citizen in South Vietnam knows that a curfew is in place from dark until dawn. Yet sometimes they take horrible risks that can result in tragic ends. I hope that such a scenario is not played-out tonight."

I checked my watch as I walked back to my CP group. The time was 2130 hours. I sat on the ground near my radio operators and leaned against a small tree. After telling both RTOs to find a quiet place and try to get some sleep, I volunteered to be on radio watch for the next two hours. I extracted a C-ration can of turkey loaf and a second can of peach slices from my backpack. It would be a cold meal, but the calories were sorely needed.

My CP was about 15 meters from the hooch. The sounds coming from the hooch were muffled. However, I could still hear an occasional screech, which I assumed came from the woman in labor. At midnight, I woke one of my RTOs to take over radio watch. As I walked back to the tree where I had left my gear, I heard a baby crying. The cry was muffled, but I could tell that it had a good set of lungs. I was curious but did not investigate. I had full confidence in my senior medic, so I laid my poncho liner on the ground and closed my eyes. I went to sleep immediately and rested well until machine gun fire startled me awake.

I checked my watch. It was 0220 hours. The sound came from the first platoon area on the larger canal. I was anxious to know the details of the action but refrained from interfering with the platoon leader. He was likely trying to do his duties and get the facts for himself. I studied the night sky for green tracers but neither saw nor heard any incoming fire. About that time, I heard the shouts, "Chieu Hoi, Chieu Hoi." An enemy soldier was yelling the words for "surrender."

My RTOs, who were still sleeping nearby, were awakened by the noise. I told them to collect their radios and gear and follow me. We walked hurriedly in the direction of the first platoon's area.

Lieutenant Khazakski met me as I neared the first platoon's

Part 1—Bizarre Things That Happen in a War Zone

ambush site, and began to speak in an excited voice. "Captain, my men in the first squad spotted two sampans traveling downstream together. The M-60 gunner was on watch at the time. He opened up on them and made quick work of both boats. There were two men in each boat. Only one survived, and he is wounded in the leg. My platoon medic is patching him up just ahead of us."

"Roger. That was some good work. Kudos to your guys. What happened to the other three?"

"They sunk into the muddy canal water with their sampans and never resurfaced. Three of my guys, including the machine gunner, watched through their night vision scopes as they went under the water. The wounded enemy managed to swim to the canal bank and my guys pulled him to safety."

"OK. Let me take a look at this guy and ask your medic about his condition. I really dislike the idea of bringing in a medevac, but it might be necessary."

I followed the lieutenant a few meters to his CP where I found the enemy soldier lying on the ground with the platoon medic finishing the wrapping on his leg. Duc was talking to the prisoner in Vietnamese. Soon after I arrived, he turned to me and began to speak.

"This man no from here, sir. He from north. I think he officer in North Vietnam Army," Duc said in his broken English.

"Why do you think he is from the north and an officer in the North Vietnam Army?"

"He no talk like us in South Vietnam. We no have shoes in South Vietnam like he have. Look at his hands, Captain. His hands are soft like officer. He no work. He make private soldier work for him," Duc concluded mirthfully.

"Thank you, Duc. What you said is very helpful."

I spoke to the platoon medic about the prisoner's condition and examined the prisoner's hands and boots as Duc had suggested. I also asked the medic for advice regarding whether the prisoner should be evacuated by helicopter. He said that the bullet passed very near the femur and may have fractured it and that the bleeding was difficult to stop. That's all I needed to convince me to call for a medevac because I considered this enemy to be a high-value prisoner.

I ordered the second platoon to send a squad to the mortar platoon to assist in securing an LZ for the medevac. When we had traveled to our ambush positions, we passed through an area the size of a

VII. A New Life

football field that had been several rice paddies that were divided by dikes. It was ideal for the helicopter to land and pick up the prisoner. By the time the medevac arrived and took the prisoner away, it was twilight. The night sounds had quieted and early morning sounds could be heard.

My RTOs and I saw the prisoner loaded onto the medevac ship and were making our way back to join other members of my CP group. I was exhausted and thinking absent-mindedly about our requirement to move to a designated area over two kilometers away by 0800 hours where we would be picked up by lift ships for airmobile operations all day.

Suddenly, sounds from the hooch attracted my attention. I looked back to see the two women adjusting their bundles on their shoulders and preparing to depart. When I saw Duc talking to them, I immediately decided to say farewell and check the new arrival.

As I neared the group, I noticed that everyone looked as tired as I felt. I wondered where the baby was until I noticed a large piece of cloth looped over the young woman's shoulder and draped down her back with a small bulge at her abdomen. I smiled at her and greeted her in my limited Vietnamese. She looked exhausted but managed a weak smile.

I turned to Duc and said, "Ask her if I can see the baby."

After he said a few words, the woman pulled the cloth open to reveal a small newborn. Upon seeing the small, helpless baby, I was reminded of the miracle of birth.

I turned to Duc again and asked, "Is it a boy or girl?"

"It is boy, Captain. She very proud. It is her first baby to live. Other babies die."

"Please tell her that I am sorry that I forced her to stay here last night. Also, tell her that I hope Buddha looks kindly on her and her baby son."

Duc dropped his cigarette on the ground and stepped on it before continuing. "She very happy, Captain. Sergeant Medina is like doctor. He know everything to do and he have many supplies to use. Also, Captain, other woman know many thing about baby. She help much."

Hearing the details helped me to perk up a bit because it had been a successful mission. We denied the enemy the use of an important transportation route; we thinned its ranks by four and

Part 1—Bizarre Things That Happen in a War Zone

captured a high-value prisoner; we sustained no casualties; and my senior medic helped a local woman birth a son safely. Last, but not least, I was grateful family or friends did not search for those women and come near our security perimeter during the night.

VIII

The Saigon Girl

It was late March 1969, and we were conducting another reconnaissance of a troublesome area a few kilometers west of the Ninth Infantry Division's base camp. We were inserted on the banks of the Mekong River by both air cushion vehicles (ACVs) and World War II–vintage landing craft. The insertion had not gone well for some men as they left the ACV and made their way to the riverbank. Very large roots, which were completely exposed over the water's surface when the tide was completely out, caused several of us to slip and fall into the water. No one drowned, but one of my radio operators came very close when he slipped under the menacing roots with all of his gear. Rescuing and resuscitating him resulted in a considerable delay. As a result of the frustrating delays, I felt that we should push hard in order to accomplish the mission and reach our target by the prescribed time.

At 1530 hours, my radio operator, whose radio was on the company frequency, drew close and said that the second platoon leader wanted to speak to me. I took the handset of his radio and called the lieutenant.

"Charlie Two Six, this is Charlie Six, over."

"Roger. My lead element on the left flank has happened upon a situation that, in his words, you just have to see for yourself, over."

"Roger, can't you just tell me about it so we can get on with our mission?"

"Roger, Charlie Six. My squad leader with that element says it's the finest-looking damn woman he's ever seen. From the way he's talking, I wouldn't be surprised if he tries to marry her on the spot, over."

This piqued my interest. Besides, I did not believe it. In all my missions in remote areas of South Vietnam such as this, I saw

Part 1—Bizarre Things That Happen in a War Zone

only middle-aged women with lots of little children, or old, toothless ones. Such women were unattractive because by the time they reached the age of 30, they were aged in appearance well beyond their actual years and usually displayed teeth, if they had them, that were severely stained a deep orange color from chewing betel nut. I wasn't totally convinced that seeing this mysterious woman was worth the effort, but I decided to go and see this putative amazing female specimen.

My command group and I slogged through the muddy rice paddies nearly 300 meters to reach the second platoon's location, which was in the midst of a cluster of crude thatched hooches. As we drew near, one of the young sergeants from the platoon met us.

He exhibited a genuine eagerness when he spoke about the woman. "Sir, there's a fine-looking woman in this house. I've never seen one like her in these small villages, but I've heard there are many like her in Saigon."

"Well, let's go in and take a look. We don't have time to waste, but I'm anxious to see this unique specimen that you're raving about."

I walked to the front of the hut, ducked my head, and entered. As I stood erect, a young woman rose from a small stool in the corner and walked toward me. Sitting next to her on another stool was an old woman.

I believe that I was both breathless and speechless. The approaching woman was tall, shapely, and stunningly beautiful. Her facial features reflected perfect symmetry, and her eyes sparkled and signaled exceptional intelligence. Her lips were full, and when she opened her mouth to speak, she flashed even white teeth. I surely felt that I had died and gone to heaven or some other wonderful place.

As she drew near, she extended her hand and said in broken English, "Hello, Dai Wee. My name Mai Nguyen."

"Do you have an identification card, Miss Nguyen?" I asked without taking my eyes from her.

The sergeant, who was still standing nearby, stepped forward and said, "I've got it, sir."

I took the card and scanned it quickly. It contained her full name, date and place of birth, and provincial capital. Despite the pleasant surprise at finding such a beauty in this remote area, along with my joy at just staring at her, I realized that there were no reasons

VIII. The Saigon Girl

to detain or question her further. I turned to exit the little hooch and continue our mission, but my curiosity was overwhelming. I couldn't get past the question, "What in the hell was she doing here, totally out of place?"

I turned and asked, "Miss Nguyen, can you tell me why you are here?"

"Yes, Dai Wee, my father, he die. Viet Cong kill him two month ago. My mother, she write paper and tell me, but I not know this before two weeks. I leave Saigon four days before today to come here. I come to this place this morning on sampan, and I must leave this day after one hours," she responded.

"Do you mean that you traveled four days to get here, and you're leaving after visiting for only a few hours?" I demanded.

"Yes, Dai Wee. I am no safe here now. I talk to you, and Viet Cong chief will know of this after Americans leave. If I stay here, I may be killed. If VC come tonight, they rape me, and maybe kill me. If ARVN [Army of the Republic of Vietnam] soldiers come, they rape me too. I must meet old mamasans after one hour, while water in canal runs fast," she explained in her broken English. I pondered her words for a few seconds.

"Oh! So you must meet the mamasans with the sampan while the water is still moving fast in the right direction? Is that what you mean?"

"Yes, Dai Wee, I must meet sampan for ride to safe place when water is running fast. I think you call it tide. I afraid, Dai Wee, because I already miss my time to meet old mamasans. I must meet sampan now, but your soldiers, they point gun at me and tell me no to leave until you come. I in danger now, and I afraid," she explained with her eyes moistening for the first time.

I pondered her words again before speaking, then asked, "Where are you supposed to meet this sampan?"

"One kilometer from here—that way," she responded as she pointed to the north. "Two mamasans be in sampan to meet me and take me to village of My Dai where I have brother. I be safe with him," she added.

I told her that we were going in that direction and that she could come along with us. I also emphasized that we had to move quickly and she must prepare to go immediately. Her eyes lit up, and she said, "Thank you, Dai Wee. Please give me one minute so I prepare and say

Part 1—Bizarre Things That Happen in a War Zone

goodbye to my mama." I turned around at that point and barked out instructions for everyone to vacate the hooch and prepare to move.

As we emerged from the hut, Sergeant Crumly, the man who first spotted her, approached me and said, "She's just a Saigon whore, Sir. Let's fuck her and leave her here. I haven't seen a piece like that in a long time. I don't think we should pass up such an opportunity. I'll even pay her for it, if you'll let me."

I was taken aback. What jolted me the most was his willingness to leave her at that little cluster of hooches after she had made it clear that she would probably be raped and killed. I didn't mince my words when I responded.

"I can't debate your claim that she's a Saigon whore. I've never seen a Saigon whore, but from descriptions I've heard, she fits the mold. However, that's not what we're all about. If you want a Saigon whore, then you'll have to go to Saigon to get one. We'll escort her to her rendezvous point and leave her there, and that's the end of it. Do I make myself clear?" I concluded with a firmness that was meant to discourage further discussion.*

When the woman emerged from the doorway to the hooch, I hardly believed it was the same person. She wore black peasant pajamas, peasant sandals, and a traditional woven straw hat. She also carried a small bundle that appeared to contain personal items. The hat was secured to her head with a woven straw string, which slipped under her chin. The string was pulled tightly to cover as much of her face as possible. I interpreted this as a tactic to disguise herself so that she could minimize the possibility of attracting attention to herself while traveling in our midst. Her attempts to hide her natural beauty were admirable, but they failed.

As soon as she joined my command group, I ordered the company to move out. We continued our movement in a northerly direction and, within about 45 minutes, reached the point that Miss

---

*For the peasantry and others who lived and farmed in remote, unprotected areas, maintaining neutrality in this protracted guerrilla war was impossible. If one wanted to survive, one must always acknowledge that "the man with the gun is the boss." When a young boy reached the age or stature that signaled that he was capable of serving as a fighter for one side or the other, he must choose or he would be killed. Young, pretty women like the "Saigon Girl" were compelled to seek the protections of the large cities. They usually had little education, and jobs in Saigon were scarce, so for survival, they often resorted to prostitution. We knew that local VC guerrillas often visited these villages at night, and a young pretty woman was not safe.

VIII. The Saigon Girl

Nguyen had described to me. The young woman's demeaner clearly signaled her relief when she spotted the two mamasans in the sampan. They exchanged what sounded like greetings, with the old woman in the front motioning for her to get into the sampan quickly.

Miss Nguyen turned to me, grabbed my hand, and bade me goodbye. She released my hand, turned quickly, and began walking hurriedly to join the women in the sampan. I didn't realize that Sergeant Crumly was nearby until he yelled, "I'll see you in Saigon, and I'll have several dollar bills in my pocket."

Part 2

When Things Go Wrong in Combat

IX

Landing Zone Wool

It was mid–January 1966, very early in my first tour in Vietnam. I was a recent addition to Company D, Second Battalion, Eighth Cavalry, First Cavalry Division as the platoon leader of the 81 mm mortar platoon.

Intelligence information shared with us indicated that a sister battalion had encountered strong resistance from an NVA unit in an area of the Central Highlands called Bong Son. Our mission was to reinforce this battalion and participate in establishing a blocking force to trap the NVA soldiers and prevent them from escaping our cordon.

My mortar platoon was inserted in LZ Wool by helicopter along with the battalion forward tactical operations center (TOC), the weapons platoon from my same company and a 105 mm artillery battery consisting of five howitzers. There were several abandoned hooches near the periphery of the LZ, which attracted my company commander's attention. Since my men were busy digging parapets for the mortars and preparing them for fire missions, he asked me to take some men from the weapons platoon and scout around our perimeter to ensure that there were no immediate threats.

I contacted the platoon sergeant of the weapons platoon and asked him to collect several of his men so we could scout around the perimeter. We chose two of the hooches that were closest to our perimeter to start with. The men searched both hooches and reported that they were clear. As we passed by the second hooch, I noticed that much of its thatched wall nearest me was missing up to three feet from the ground. Peering in, I saw only a simple wooden frame with slats across it which appeared to be used as a bed. Under it, I noticed what appeared to be a hole. I did not approach the hooch because the troops ahead of me had already reported it clear, and the threat of booby traps in such a place discouraged unnecessary movement in or around it. We continued scouting the perimeter for another 50 meters when I just happened to glance back at the hooch with the hole under the bed. I thought I detected movement under the wooden bed, so I continued to focus on it. I could hardly believe what occurred. A nearly naked man, with what appeared to be a rifle, crawled from the hole under the bed and began dragging himself toward a nearby thicket as fast as possible. When I wheeled around and raised my M-16 rifle to my shoulder, the platoon sergeant saw my actions and followed suit. We fired our weapons nearly simultaneously. The man began flailing around, yelling "Chieu Hoi," which are the Vietnamese words for "surrender." It was evident that at least one of our bullets found its mark.

We began walking toward the wounded man slowly and cautiously with our rifles trained on him. The platoon sergeant yelled a command for one of his men to call for the platoon medic. When we drew near the man, it was evident that what appeared to be a rifle was actually a stick that he was using to assist in standing or walking. It was then that I assessed his physical condition and realized why he was dragging himself across the ground. He had small fragmentation wounds over much of his right side, and we had added to his misery by shooting him with a bullet that passed through at least one of his buttocks. The medic soon arrived and began to treat his wounds. Once the initial triage was accomplished, we placed him on the crude wooden bed from the hooch and transported him close to the battalion TOC.

The battalion intelligence officer expressed a keen interest in the prisoner and brought the Vietnamese translator to interrogate him. I was standing several feet away from the prisoner when the translator began speaking to him.

There were several verbal exchanges within five to 10 minutes before the translator turned to the intelligence officer to render the translation. "He tell me he is farmer and he live close by, but he lie. He can no hide his talk from me. I know he is from north near Hanoi. He is North Vietnamese Army officer. He is lieutenant in infantry unit. His unit had fight with American unit late yesterday in that direction on side of mountain." He stopped translating long enough to point to the west where a small mountain stood maybe 600–700 feet high. After pointing, he continued interrogating the prisoner. After several more minutes, he began translating again.

IX. Landing Zone Wool

Wounded North Vietnamese Army officer soon after being detected and shot. After interrogation, he was flown by helicopter to an evacuation hospital for treatment. Mid-January 1966.

"He think he was hit with shrapnel from American gun that shoots grenade. He say he try to go to Vietnamese farm for help, but Americans come in sky machine, so he hide in old house. He say he want to run away, but his leg hurt. No can walk. He say many Americans dead on mountain." The battalion intelligence officer drew away from the wounded enemy and directed his assistant to remain while he went to the battalion TOC to brief the battalion commander on the information gleaned from the interrogation. By this time, the medic had treated the wounds and stopped the bleeding in the man's buttocks. In the meantime, the prisoner was lying on the ground still wearing very little clothing.

Part 2—When Things Go Wrong in Combat

I took advantage of the temporary pause in the interrogation to ask a question about an issue that continued to haunt me. I turned to the translator and asked, "Why didn't my men see this man in the hole under the bed when they checked it? Were they careless or is there some other reason?"

The translator spent an additional five minutes questioning the prisoner before he turned to me once more. "He say hole goes down and back. He make move with hands like letter *L* in English. American soldiers can no see him in back part of hole." Other Americans call this "spider hole."

That was my introduction to the "spider hole." We encountered many more such holes before my tour ended. They were generally too narrow for Americans to fit into for inspection. Such holes, with the "L" segment several feet underground, were good protection from bombardment by artillery or bombs dropped from aircraft.

The intelligence officer returned after about 15 minutes and stated that he had requested a medevac. Additionally, he requested that some of the men from the weapons platoon be available to transport the wounded prisoner to the helicopter. The medevac arrived within about 20 minutes, and that was the end of our excitement—at least, we thought so.

As I turned to walk back to the mortar platoon, my radio operator intercepted me and reported that Captain Butner, who was my company commander, requested my presence at his CP. Sergeant First Class Hanson, who was the acting platoon leader of the weapons platoon, joined me as I walked toward my commander's CP.

When we reached the CP, Captain Butner wasted no time in explaining the issue at hand. "A sister battalion, which is located about two kilometers to our north, has been in this area for several days. In fact, their recon unit is the one that first encountered the NVA unit that is, or was, on the side of the mountain to the west of us. Their recon platoon walked into a classic V-shaped ambush late yesterday and had several men either killed or wounded. They know that 14 men were either killed on the side of that mountain or separated from their unit and scattered in the jungle. Sixteen men of the platoon managed to escape the ambush because they were trailing in the rear of the formation. Some of them were wounded but managed to make it out alive and report the details of the ambush. The unit has requested help in bringing their dead and wounded down from

IX. Landing Zone Wool

A wounded North Vietnamese Army soldier. He was shot by our reconnaissance platoon while trying to escape through our lines. He was evacuated to an evacuation hospital soon after this photograph was taken. Mid-January 1966.

the mountainside so that they can be loaded out on medevacs. We're the closest to them from our battalion, so we're going to send the entire weapons platoon with you in charge, Lieutenant. Be ready to move out in 20 minutes. It's likely that the NVA unit has withdrawn from that particular area because some of their men have been killed while trying to escape through American lines. According to the NVA prisoner, they fled out of fear of an American bombardment

Part 2—When Things Go Wrong in Combat

by artillery and aircraft. I hope they've evacuated the area, but don't take it for granted. Be prepared to defend yourselves, and be very mindful of the potential for booby traps. Any questions?"

My curiosity prompted me to ask, "Sir, I'm anxious to learn if we know what time of the day this unit encountered the ambush?"

Captain Butner glanced at his notes before speaking. "The information provided indicates that the engagement took place just before dark yesterday, so it's been roughly 16 hours. That's what you'll be dealing with, so I don't expect it to be pretty. Just be respectful and helpful. I know that the members of the unit must be feeling pretty dejected at this point. There's great concern about the status of the equipment that was in the possession of the men who were killed. They fear that two M-60 machine guns, at least one night vision sight, one PRC-25 radio, and several M-16 rifles could have been taken by the enemy."

My commander handed me a piece of paper with the grid coordinates of the site on the side of the mountain. After a quick map analysis, I determined that our target area was a distance of about one and a half kilometers to the west. After careful preparation, we walked through our perimeter and joined a 20-man group from the sister battalion, which brought our number to 45. The other group was led by a first lieutenant, so I deferred to him for primary leadership. He reassured me about security when he placed his men on line with a point man leading the way about 10 meters ahead of the main group. We provided rear security, separated at a distance of about 20 meters from his group. We made good time until we had covered about 500 meters, at which time the jungle surface became very slippery. It was the rainy season, and true to form, it was raining lightly.

We encountered no enemy resistance or booby traps. As we approached the ambush site, it became eerily quiet. Some of the men from the sister unit wept as they recognized their friends among the dead. I asked Sergeant First Class Hanson to take several of his men and cut saplings that could be used to make improvised litters.

I finally made my way to the upper part of the draw where the lead elements of the ill-fated platoon had become victims of the ambush. The other lieutenant was issuing orders to make improvised litters, just as I had done. Several feet from the corpse of the soldier I took to be the point man, I noticed that the body nearest me had a subdued lieutenant's bar on the lapel of his jungle fatigues.

IX. Landing Zone Wool

We were collecting any valuables that we could find, so I checked the lieutenant's pockets for his wallet. Failing to find it on his person, I extended my search to the surrounding area and soon found it on the ground nearby. Upon opening the wallet, I found only some pictures. Leafing through the photos, I suddenly got a sick feeling because I recognized the lieutenant. He had been a fellow student in paratrooper training at Fort Benning, Georgia, in April of the previous year. I also remembered that he was a West Point graduate, so I checked his hands for his class ring. Finding that the ring finger on his right hand had been severed, I felt a mix of emotion from anger to revulsion. The pilferers had also extracted his molars, which probably contained fillings. I delivered the wallet to the other lieutenant who was also collecting valuables. All rings and watches had been removed from the bodies by the enemy soldiers. Other soldiers' mouths were gaping open where the enemy had removed any tooth that appeared to contain valuable metal. Boots had been removed from most bodies, and all of the weapons and other equipment had been hauled away.

We spent nearly an hour preparing a sufficient number of improvised litters to accommodate all of the dead. It was a treacherous and arduous trek back to LZ Wool, what with the weight of the bodies and slippery trails leading off the mountain.

The entire battalion spent several more days as part of the blocking force to prevent the NVA soldiers from escaping. The reconnaissance platoon wounded a lone NVA soldier and brought him into our perimeter for interrogation and medical treatment. I considered this tragic experience part of my education that would continue for another 11 months.

X

The Orangutan Caper

In the spring of 1966, my unit was part of an air assault into the eastern part of the mountainous Central Highlands of South Vietnam. I was assigned as the leader of the 81 mm mortar platoon of Company D, Second Battalion, Eighth Cavalry. As usual, my mortar platoon was co-located with the forward-deployed battalion CP, which was comprised of the battalion commander and much of his principal staff. When forward deployed, it required security because the enemy threat encompassed 360 degrees. The enemy forces spent much of their time and energy ensuring that absolute security was rarely achievable for U.S. forces.

It was routine practice to deploy a 105 mm artillery battery, consisting of five guns, with the battalion headquarters. Much of the time, men from the artillery and men from my mortar platoon were the sole providers of perimeter security. Occasionally, the reconnaissance platoon and the heavy weapons platoon, which were also assigned to my parent company, would be available to augment security. Thinning our ranks for security duty taxed the ability of my mortar platoon and the 105 mm artillery battery to conduct our primary mission of providing indirect fire support.

We had recently terminated a deployment to the western area of the Central Highlands, where we operated north of Pleiku in the vicinity of Kontum and Pleime. The malaria threat was such that several men of my platoon had been evacuated suffering from the effects of this dreaded disease. Fortunately, before we departed the First Cavalry Division base camp for the current mission, we had received five new replacements.

The battalion operations officer had chosen a knoll on which to deploy the battalion forward CP for this particular mission. The knoll was treeless but covered with dried, waist-high sage grass.

X. The Orangutan Caper

The reconnaissance platoon, the heavy weapons platoon with its 50-caliber machine guns and 106 mm recoilless anti-tank guns, and my mortar platoon were inserted by helicopter on the knoll first and were followed soon by the 105 mm artillery battery. As soon as we conducted sweeps around the area to verify that it was secure, the battalion commander, his abbreviated staff, and a support group from the battalion headquarters company arrived by helicopters.

Within the hour, the recon platoon departed the area with a mission that would require four to five days to complete. The senior men of the 105 mm howitzer battery and my mortar platoon began "laying" the guns to ensure that they were ready to conduct fire missions. My platoon sergeant placed two men about 200 meters to the east of the knoll in a listening post and placed six men in two-man positions on our part of the perimeter. As soon as possible, everyone began digging foxholes. My platoon sergeant, my radio operator, and I dug a three-man hole together. Once it was completed, we three entered the hole to ensure that we could fit into it completely. By the time we finished, our foxhole was nearly large enough to accommodate a Volkswagen. There was a real and constant enemy threat from rocket-propelled grenades, Katyusha rockets, mortars, and light artillery.

As darkness approached, my platoon sergeant recalled the two men on the listening post and posted two of the new men in an additional position on our part of the perimeter. As the two new men dug a foxhole, I overheard them chatting about their plan to have one man on watch while the other slept nearby.

As the sun disappeared over the horizon, the usual blanket of darkness fell all around, and, with the exception the blasts of occasional harassment and interdiction rounds launched from both the 105 mm guns and the 81 mm mortars, quiet prevailed. As usual, my platoon sergeant and I checked every position on our part of the perimeter to ensure that the men had set claymore mines in front of their positions, that their individual rifles were loaded, and that they had several handheld flares.

Everything was quiet and normal until about 2200 hours, when one of the new men fired a handheld flare. Within seconds, a loud explosion followed as he ignited the claymore mine in front of his position. This was followed by automatic weapons fire, not from one man but from both men in that position. As the first flare parachuted

Part 2—When Things Go Wrong in Combat

closer to the ground, they fired another one. By this time, my platoon sergeant and I had run part of the distance to the position and crawled the remaining 10 meters.

"What have you got out there?" I queried loudly as I approached.

"Jacobelly was on watch, sir. He claims that he saw two Viet Cong in uniform and that one of them had an AK-47 rifle and a pack. They ran back that way," the nervous soldier stated as he pointed to the north.

"I neither heard nor saw an incoming round. Did they shoot at you?"

"I don't think so, Sir. As soon as Jacobelly fired the first flare, they started running."

I then directed my comments to the man who had been on watch. "Do you think that you hit them with either your claymore or with small-arms fire?"

"I don't know, Sir. I think they were already past the claymore when I fired it, and I doubt that I hit them with my M-16 because they were hard to see when they slumped down in the tall grass."

"OK. One of you come to the platoon CP and get another claymore and a couple more flares," I stated as I turned to leave the position.

"Sergeant Gomez, go back to the platoon CP and place everyone on high alert. I have to go directly to the battalion CP and report this incident. It's potentially serious because it could have been a probing action and the enemy was clumsy at it," I said as I began walking hurriedly in the direction of the battalion CP.

As I approached the medium-size tent that housed the battalion commander and his staff, I met the officer from the artillery battery who was responsible for security. I explained in detail what had transpired on the perimeter to the battalion commander, several of his staff members, and others who were present in the tent. I also volunteered that my entire platoon would be in a higher state of readiness for the next couple of hours in the event this was a probing incident and more enemy action might follow. I also requested to be relieved of the task of firing harassment and interdiction fires all night so that I could place more men on the perimeter. My request was granted.

Things returned to a state of normalcy until shortly after midnight. The men in the same position fired a handheld flare. It was followed by the explosion from one of their claymore mines and several

X. The Orangutan Caper

volleys of automatic weapons fire. My platoon sergeant and I raced toward the position—crawling the last 10 meters for fear that we were being attacked. The situation was an exact repeat of the first with no enemy rounds coming into our perimeter. One of the men swore that he saw two VC fighters with AK-47 rifles in their hands. Furthermore, he swore that he hit one of the enemy soldiers when he shot his M-16 rifle.

As I again walked hurriedly to the battalion CP, I thought to myself that any mention of my soldier's statement that he shot one of the enemy soldiers would precipitate an order to sweep the area outside of our perimeter. My prediction was amazingly accurate. After listening to my report, the battalion commander asked two questions. The first was, "Did anyone see or hear any enemy fire coming into our perimeter?" and "Did anyone other than the two men in the one position identify enemy soldiers?" When I answered no to both questions, he ordered a sweep of the area.

After returning to my CP, I told my platoon sergeant to leave men in all positions on the east side of the perimeter and gather 20 men to sweep the west side of the grassy knoll. Before moving into position to conduct the sweep, I requested an illumination mission from a 105 mm artillery battery that was about five kilometers to our southwest. When the battery fired the first round, it did not illuminate the area well. After the forward observer ordered an adjustment, the light from the following rounds penetrated the grass perfectly so that we could see into it.

After briefing everyone on our plan to sweep the area, my platoon sergeant spread men westward every three to five meters, and I took the east flank. I instructed one of the men, who reported seeing the intruders and firing on them, to lead the group in the direction the enemy soldiers had fled. We all proceeded very slowly as successive artillery illumination rounds were fired overhead. Suddenly, one of the men to my left called out, "I found one." Then the man next to him called out, "Here's the other one, too. They ain't Viet Cong, though. They're big gorillas."

Upon hearing this information, I had a flood of emotions. Relief, anger, and embarrassment all flooded my senses at the same time. I dreaded having to be the one to report that there were no enemy soldiers—simply two orangutans that were probably trying to return to their traditional nesting area.

Part 2—When Things Go Wrong in Combat

My platoon sergeant and I learned a valuable lesson, which prompted me to institute a policy of never placing two new men in the same position at night if they were from the city and had not been exposed to the sights and sounds of a forest or jungle.

While the senior officers in my chain of command understood what had happened, they were still disturbed at the fate of the innocent wild animals. I was told in no uncertain terms that my men and I must dig graves and bury the unlucky critters. We dug appropriately sized holes the following morning and made some crude crosses from nearby saplings. Once we had covered the two graves, one of my men, who had earned the reputation of platoon clown, requested to say a few words. He removed his steel helmet and held it over his heart before speaking. At first, we thought he was going to be serious for once when he said, "May God give these poor critters peace." Then, after a short pause, he said, "Ashes to ashes, dust to dust, and fuzz that wuzz." It goes without saying that most of my platoon members and I were compelled to laugh at his lighthearted commentary.

XI

Kicked Out Two Stories Up

It was late spring of 1966 and I was the leader of an 81 mm mortar platoon in a subordinate company of the First Cavalry Division (Airmobile). Our mission on that particular day would take us to an area where the intelligence officials of the division reported recent activity by North Vietnamese regulars.

I lined up my platoon members in groups of six in a staggered line for pickup by the UH-1 helicopters. Because the entire first brigade of the division was designated as an airborne unit, every piece of equipment that was assigned to us was "air droppable." Therefore, once we departed the helicopters, we were "foot soldiers."

To not overload any of my soldiers, the four mortars in the platoon were disassembled into five components: outer ring of the base plate, inner ring of the base plate, tube (47 inches long), bipod, and sight. Excluding weight, the most cumbersome component to carry in the jungle was the tube. It was traditionally carried on a man's back perpendicular to his body. Many jungle trails and paths were narrow, and a tube nearly four feet long was always impacting nearby vegetation. Mortar crew members were expected to carry a major mortar component plus their individual weapon, ammunition, and gear (water, food, and personal items). Crew members, who were not loaded with mortar components, carried two or three mortar rounds on their backs as well as their individual weapons and gear. Helicopter pilots had commented on previous occasions that mortar crewmen were considered to be heavy and required the pilots and crew to be especially attentive to the effect of air density on the helicopter's lift capabilities.

I wasn't thinking about any of these factors as my platoon sergeant, my radio operator, and I climbed into one side of the helicopter as three of my mortar crewmen climbed into the other side. The choppers had just arrived, with their turbine engines humming at

Part 2—When Things Go Wrong in Combat

a high pitch and their main rotors beating at the late-morning air. None of us combat troops sat on any seats for these airmobile operations. Instead, we sat on the floor of the chopper with our backs to the middle and our feet dangling over the skids so that we could exit quickly and easily and so that we could fire at the enemy from that position if necessary.

It was a long ride from the First Air Cavalry Division base camp near the small village of An Khe to the area known as Bong Son, which was familiar to most of us. My platoon members had filled the first five choppers that arrived to transport us to our exit point. The chopper in which I rode was in the middle of the single file of five with two in front with mortarmen and two more following. The battalion commander and his operations officer had already reached the new LZ in the command-and-control helicopter and directed artillery fire on it. The artillery fire would be lifted only seconds before we would arrive in the choppers.

As we neared the targeted strip of land, the choppers began to descend. They were traveling at a safe distance apart in single file. We grunts would often stand on the chopper's skids and leap from them as soon as the craft was within several feet of the ground.

We were still too far from the LZ to slip onto the skids, so I focused my attention on the two lead choppers. I watched as my platoon members slipped onto the skids of the lead chopper as it approached the LZ. When it was within several feet of the grassy area, they began to leap from the aircraft. As soon as the troops had departed the chopper, it rotated forward and began to climb back to altitude. What happened next caused a chain reaction that defied explanation initially.

Instead of running from the small LZ as was our usual practice, the men remained on the small grassy plot and began removing their gear in what appeared to be a panic mode. They then huddled around the part of the grassy plot where the men on the left side of the chopper exited. To me, this was incomprehensible behavior.

The immediate effect forced the chopper in line to land next, and the choppers behind it, including ours, to stop in midair and hover. The small LZ could accommodate only one chopper at a time. This was potentially a disastrous situation because several choppers in this single file were too far from the ground, and the immediate environs were not suitable for landing helicopters.

XI. Kicked Out Two Stories Up

Suddenly, my attention was drawn to a beeping sound in the chopper in which we were riding. I soon realized that this sound was coming from the console in front of the pilot. It was accompanied by a flashing red light that I interpreted to mean that the chopper was in crisis. I heard the small turbine engine groaning and sensed that the main rotor was not beating the air at the same frequency. The pilot turned toward the rear of the chopper and spoke frantically into his microphone, after which the door gunner moved farther toward the back of the helicopter. I looked ahead at the lead chopper to see it wobbling from side to side. It was losing altitude slowly, as was ours.

Suddenly, I felt a hard impact on my back as the door gunner planted his foot in the middle of my backpack and pushed me from the helicopter. I managed to push from the skid with my left foot just enough to point my feet toward the ground. This caused me to land very hard on my left side with my leg collapsing immediately and my knee impacting the ground. I crashed into the ground with something hitting me in the mouth hard enough to force my lower teeth through my lip.

I rolled onto my back to assess my condition. Before trying to stand, I moved both legs and rose to my feet slowly. The taste of blood was strong, but I could no longer think of my own troubles because my radio operator was screaming, "I can't feel my legs. Somebody help me. I can't feel my legs and I can't move. Help! Help!" I walked very unsteadily several feet to his location and cringed. The poor soldier had fallen on his back onto his radio. At nearly the same time, my platoon sergeant crawled to our location. When our eyes met, there was clear recognition on both our parts that this young soldier was in serious trouble.

"Do you know, Sir, if the door gunner succeeded in pushing the men from the other side of the chopper?"

"No, I don't. I don't hear any voices near us. Let's try and remove the radio from underneath Private Williams to see if it works. We've gotta request a medevac immediately."

We managed to remove the radio and were extremely relieved to determine that it worked flawlessly. I notified my company commander of the situation and requested a medevac. I also asked him to send four men as litter bearers, and a medic to my location so that Private Williams could be carried to an open area big enough to accommodate a medevac chopper.

Part 2—When Things Go Wrong in Combat

In the meantime, we heard a crashing sound as the chopper from which we had descended crashed into the brush between us and the LZ. By this time of the day, the temperature had risen to 90 degrees, and that temperature combined with the high humidity had pushed the air density to a high level. It was a well-known fact that these single-engine helicopters struggled with hovering for long periods in such conditions, especially when loaded with heavy troops.

At that time, the sergeant and the two men who rode in the other side of the same chopper came crashing through the brush. As soon as he arrived, the sergeant asked, "Are y'all all right? We could hear someone screaming the length of a football field away."

"No, the platoon sergeant and I are slightly injured, but Private Williams landed on his radio, injuring his back. I've requested a medevac, and we're going to need help taking him out of here by litter. Please stick around just in case we need you three to help. Did the door gunner kick you out, too?"

"No, sir. After we saw what he did to you, we grabbed his legs and pulled him down to the floor. We stayed in the chopper until it was close to the ground, then we jumped out because we didn't want to go down with it. Do you have any idea what happened on the LZ to make our guys act the way they did?"

"No, I don't. They caused one hell of a problem when they stayed on the LZ. I can't even speculate. It must have been very serious to cause them to do what they did."

Suddenly, my attention was drawn to my company commander's voice on the radio. "Vilseck Three, this is Vilseck Six, over."

"This is Vilseck Three, over."

"This is Vilseck Six. A medevac chopper is inbound. We've cleared an alternate LZ about 100 meters north of the original one. That's where the men should take your injured man. I'm about to dispatch four men with a litter and a medic to your location. Please pop yellow smoke so they can find you. By the way, do not walk on the original LZ for any reason. It's a thick grassy mat that's floating on the top of a deep body of water. It's deceptive and looks like grass growing on the ground. That's why one of your men—the one carrying a mortar tube—broke through it when he jumped from the first chopper. Some of your men stripped off their gear and dove down to free him from his equipment and gear and help him back to the surface. He took in some water but will be OK. I know their rescue effort

XI. Kicked Out Two Stories Up

caused a big problem, but a man's life was hanging in the balance. They had no choice, and I'm immensely proud of them. By the way, is anyone else injured? I heard that you and your platoon sergeant took bad falls from the chopper. Are you two injured?"

"We're banged up a bit but will be OK with a little mending. My radio operator has what appears to be a life-altering injury and needs to get to an evac hospital as quickly as possible. Thanks for ordering the medevac. Everyone is doing everything possible at this point to help him. We're grateful."

Within about 20 minutes, the men with the litter and the medic arrived and began to lift Private Williams onto it. My platoon sergeant and I accompanied the litter crew. I had not traveled far when I realized that the pain in my left knee was causing me difficulty stepping over obstacles. The pain became so severe that it prompted me to examine my knee, at which time I saw that it was badly bruised and swollen. After the foursome transported Private Williams to the medevac and he was securely onboard the chopper, we walked another 400 meters to the place where we would set up the mortars and prepare for any fire missions that might be called in. As usual, we were co-located with the battalion forward CP and were part of the security for that headquarters.

I called on the senior medic who usually accompanied the battalion forward CP and asked him to examine my knee. He opined that it was a bad sprain and wrapped it with an elastic bandage. It was so severely swollen that I could not bend it more than just a few degrees, so I was unable to lead patrols for more than three weeks. It took that long for the swelling to recede to the point that I could travel through the jungle without stumbling over simple obstacles. In the meantime, my lip healed within about 10 days. However, I will never get over my distrust of door gunners.

XII

A Lot of Bull

In May 1966, I was the platoon leader of an 81 mm mortar platoon that was part of Company D, Second Battalion, Eighth Cavalry, First Cavalry Division. My platoon had the mission of conducting a daylight reconnaissance around a forward operating base. Inside the base was our battalion forward CP with the battalion commander and some of his staff, a 105 mm howitzer battery with five howitzers, and my mortar platoon with four 81 mm mortars. Also inside the base was an LZ with frequent helicopter traffic. We were operating in the Central Highlands of South Vietnam in an area that was referred to as Bong Son. The topography was mountainous with tall jungle canopy.

When we remained in a static position in the jungle for more than two days, standing policy required us to conduct a reconnaissance to ensure that the enemy was not consolidating forces for a major attack on us. We departed the perimeter of the base early that morning to beat the heat and humidity, which usually became a serious factor by 0930 hours. It was a given that existing trails were booby-trapped; therefore, we were forced sometimes to make our way through dense undergrowth. This condition caused us to cut our way frequently with machetes and walk in single file.

The length of the route that we were required to check was about five kilometers. By midmorning, we had covered only about 2,000 meters, and conditions were already uncomfortable under the tall canopy. An examination of my map showed a stream ahead, and when we came to it, I ordered a short break. For security, I sent two men 100 meters in the direction of travel and two toward the rear. We filled our canteens with the cool, clear water and added purification tablets, then rested for a few minutes. After a short break, we swapped out the men on security so that they could replenish their canteens and relax a few minutes.

XII. A Lot of Bull

My recon patrol consisted of 16 men, including my radio operator and me. I had left 14 men behind in the forward base to man two of our four mortars in the event the mortar platoon was called on to fire support missions. In this long, single file, there were 10 men in front of my radio operator and me and four men bringing up rear security. Each man was separated by five meters from the man in front and the one behind him. This policy was essential to minimize casualties from booby traps, mines, and possible ambush.

After traveling another 1,000 meters we came to a low area. There was no running water, but the ground was moist and the air felt cool. Our pace had slowed because the moisture encouraged a lot of undergrowth, and my point man was forced to use the machete frequently to cut a trail. The area was actually quite attractive with some very large, tall trees and lots of welcome shade.

Suddenly, there was a loud crashing sound to my right front. I instinctively brought my M-16 rifle to my right shoulder and placed my right index finger in the trigger slot and my thumb on the firing selector. The source of the sound made its way to our column about 15 meters ahead of me. I saw a large black blur and then heard one of my soldiers scream in agony. I could not identify the attacker until the animal turned around and charged another soldier closer to me. The second soldier saw the water buffalo charging in time to run behind a large tree, which enabled him to dodge the raging bull. Another, who was ahead of me in the column, began shooting at the bull. I yelled for him to cease firing and ordered that no one but me was to shoot at the animal. I was fearful that we would accidentally shoot one another if I permitted everyone to shoot randomly.

When the bull moved to either side of the trail in his attempts to gore more soldiers, I shot him repeatedly with my M-16 rifle, leaving my selector on semiautomatic to increase accuracy. Because the bullets merely ricocheted from his head, I aimed for his eyes when he was facing me. I rarely had a shot at him standing broadside, but when I did, I shot for his heart. After the raging animal finally dropped to its knees and collapsed, I determined that I had fired 70 rounds at him. There were many rips in his hide where the M-16 rounds had impacted but did not penetrate his thick hide sufficiently to be lethal. After he fell, I said a silent prayer because this half-ton animal had appeared determined to kill as many of us as possible.

After treating the injured soldier, the medic reported that he

Part 2—When Things Go Wrong in Combat

sustained probable broken ribs and a possible punctured lung from the vicious attack. He rated the victim's condition as serious and opined that he must be evacuated as soon as possible. Other soldiers were already busy cutting saplings with which to make a litter. After reporting the casualty to the battalion operations center and requesting a medevac, I studied my map, looking for the nearest area that appeared clear enough to land a helicopter. I identified an area that was about 200 meters from the site of the attack.

Within a few minutes, several soldiers had assembled the improvised litter from saplings and a poncho, as we had learned in our training. The trip to the cleared area was very difficult, with the point man cutting the trail the entire way. We all took turns carrying the litter because it was very exhausting, and the heat and humidity were smothering at that time of the day.

Within about 20 minutes, we heard the beat of the helicopter blades, and I began speaking to the pilot on my platoon radio. I gave him the coordinates of the cleared area, which was only about 30 meters ahead of us. As soon as we reached the clearing, my radio operator activated one of his smoke grenades. I sent men to the edges of the cleared area for security, and the medevac landed on our smoke. I was very relieved to see the chopper lift off safely with our injured fellow soldier.

We completed our reconnaissance mission by 1500 hours that afternoon without further incident. If my soldiers wrote home that night to parents, siblings, wives, and girlfriends, they surely included stories about a lot of bull.

XIII

The Unsent Letter

It was late November 1968 and I had been in command of a rifle company for slightly over a month. We conducted a company-size air assault mission into an area that was described as an active VC target, so we were prepared to find probable enemy resistance upon landing. The targeted area was located close to a large canal that had clusters of peasant hooches on both sides and several large sampans tied near both banks.

I sent my first platoon to search the hooches on the near bank and kept the other two rifle platoons in a position to support the first platoon, if needed. The first platoon completed the search, and the platoon leader reported that they had found nothing suspicious among the hooches. I was about to order a withdrawal from the area when my battalion commander contacted me by radio and ordered me to send several men to check the sampans that were next to the near bank. I acknowledged his order and instructed my third platoon, which was on my right flank, to send several men to conduct the search. My CP group and I were on a knoll 50–75 meters from the canal bank, so I had a good view of the area.

As the three men approached within approximately 20 meters of the big canal, several enemy fighters engaged them from the opposite riverbank with automatic AK-47 fire. Then they turned their rifles on my CP group and me. I heard the call immediately for a medic from the three soldiers near the riverbank. All three of the men were shot and crawling for cover. I noticed right away that one of the men was crawling with great effort and yelling for a medic. The enemy was still spraying the whole area, including the knoll where my CP group was situated. As soon as the remainder of the third platoon opened fire on the enemy, the enemy fire decreased but did not cease completely.

Part 2—When Things Go Wrong in Combat

In the meantime, my senior medic was crawling to the wounded soldiers while being targeted by the enemy fighters across the canal, but he was not deterred. The corporal, who led the trio to conduct the search of the sampans, finally made his way to my location. The third platoon medic came to the corporal's aid and discovered that he had a sucking chest wound. While being treated, the corporal shared his observation that one of the other two men was losing a lot of blood from a bullet wound to his upper leg.

I requested a medevac and instructed my forward observer to call for artillery fire. It was impossible to cross such a large canal without subjecting ourselves to grave risk. The artillery fire soon persuaded the enemy fighters to flee the area.

Two of the three wounded were ambulatory. Members of the third platoon made a litter from a poncho and some saplings that they used to bring the third wounded soldier close to my location. The medic had injected an intravenous drip into his arm and placed a tourniquet on his leg to stop the bleeding. He told me that he had injected him with morphine to help calm him. I pulled the medic far enough away from the wounded men to ask for a succinct description of the wounds and prognosis.

"Corporal Hayslip has a sucking chest wound, which is serious, but I'm confident that he'll make it. The private with them has a flesh wound. I don't consider his wound life threatening. Corporal Manchewski's wound is very serious because the bullet broke his femur and severed the artery. He lost a lot of blood before I could reach him. He is already in shock, so his survival is questionable at best. Unless the medevac arrives very quickly, he doesn't stand a good chance of making it, sir."

I gave my battalion commander a summary of what transpired. As I was delivering my report, the medevac arrived and the wounded soldiers were loaded onboard for transport to the evacuation hospital in the Ninth Infantry Division base camp.

Those of us familiar with the nature and extent of Corporal Manchewski's wounds knew that he was in serious danger. His likable personality and quick wit endeared him to all of us, so we looked for reasons to believe that he would survive. After all, the medic had made his way to him as quickly as possible, stopped the bleeding, and started the blood expander drip in time to save him. At least, that is what we wanted to believe.

XIII. The Unsent Letter

In midafternoon, we were airlifted out of that area and inserted within a couple of kilometers of two canals that we would ambush overnight.

We did not get the news of Corporal "Ski's" death until later that night. I called the third platoon leader and asked him to come to my location. I took him aside and informed him of "Ski's" death, and asked him to not inform his men until the following morning because I expected such news to spread like a wildfire. I also instructed the members of my CP group to keep the news under wraps until the following morning.

The next day, we were airlifted to the Ninth Division base camp for a two-day stand-down. There was a lot of murmuring among the troops about Corporal Manchewski's death. Later in the day, the third platoon leader spoke to me regarding concerns among his men that incompetence or unacceptable delays in his treatment caused his death. He emphasized that some of the men insisted that he should not have died.

I was deeply troubled and saddened at such claims, so I went to the hospital to get firsthand information from the staff. A doctor, who was present in the intensive care unit (ICU) when Corporal Manchewski arrived by medevac, met me and spoke about the young soldier. He said that the wounded soldier was in deep shock upon arrival due to the loss of blood. He emphasized that a full medical crew tried desperately to save him, but several vital organs were already shutting down upon his arrival. This was not my first time to hear such an explanation. Such thoughts did not, however, lessen the sadness that I felt for this young American's family.

I was an abysmal failure at shutting out the tendency to revisit the incidents that resulted in my fellow Americans suffering serious wounds or death while following my orders. Likewise, I could never escape the reality that every soldier who died in the war zone would be remembered, loved, and mourned by someone "back home." Every time the dreaded army sedan stopped at someone's home and the occupants heard the knock on the door, their pulse surely quickened and their throat tightened. The reality was that the pain lingered a very long time because the empty chair at the dinner table was a constant reminder of the loss of someone who could never be replaced.

Part 2—When Things Go Wrong in Combat

Two Weeks Later

The battalion chaplain notified me that he would conduct a memorial service at 10 o'clock the next day. I felt strongly about attending the service, so I arrived a few minutes early. The small chapel was packed with more soldiers than I had ever seen at one of these services. A large number of men from my company was in attendance to honor and respect our fallen fellow soldier. The chaplain led the group in singing "Amazing Grace," which was a common practice at such events. That song evokes acute sadness when I hear it—even today, some 56 years later.

After the service, I returned to my company area to find that there had been a mail delivery and I was the recipient of several letters. I naturally thumbed through them, looking at the return addresses with great anticipation. One return address left me dreading to open the envelope because it contained Corporal Manchewski's family name.

After opening and reading two letters from my family members, I finally found the courage to open the dreaded one. The letter was from his mother; it was tactful, reflecting language and composition of a well-educated person. She stated that some of the men who were in the same platoon with her son had written to her. In their letters, they had expressed dismay at the medical chain's inability to save her son's life. She even hinted at incompetence and untimeliness on the part of the attending combat medic as a possible cause of her son's death. I was very troubled at the content and tone of her letter, so I spent several hours composing a letter in which I explained in detail the circumstances under which the brave medic crawled to her son's rescue and did everything possible at that level to stabilize him. I told her of my admiration and respect for her young son and how I grieved at his loss. I was on the cusp of mailing the letter when I suddenly realized that I had best get my superior's approval. Such situations, if mishandled, could lead to a dreaded congressional investigation.

I requested to see the battalion commander and was able to take the letter to him the same afternoon. He read the letter quickly, placed it facedown on his desk, and stared at me for a few seconds—making me feel very uncomfortable.

He said, "Tell me every detail as to what motivated you to write

XIII. The Unsent Letter

this grieving mother." I handed him her letter, which he read quickly and handed back to me.

He leaned back in the chair with his arms folded across his chest, causing me to sense that things were not going well. "George, I know that you mean well. You're a very compassionate person, and that's a trait that I admire in you. Your heartfelt sadness for this young soldier is clearly evident in your letter, and I believe that his mother could benefit from the detail that you included in your comments. I must emphasize to you, though, that you may not send this letter. The division Judge Advocate General's office is the single source for answering such communications. That is a hard-and-fast rule, and should you forward this letter, there could be an inexplicable backlash if she were to write to her congressman asking him to investigate the matter."

I was quick but respectful in my appeal. "But, sir, you know that she'll get a cold form-letter that won't satisfy her. In fact, it will only tell her what she already knows. She needs closure on the one hand, and she needs to know that everyone in the medical chain worked diligently to save her son's life, on the other hand."

"I know what you mean, George, and if it makes you feel any better, I agree with you. However, this is a rule that if broken could be career ending for you and me. Just leave her letter with me and instruct the men in your company that they are to be more mindful of their comments to the parents of fallen soldiers. Thank you for caring so much, but those are the rules."

The next day, I assembled the entire third platoon in front of the company and explained the impact of their letters to Corporal Manchewski's parents. I revealed first that I had received the letter from the fallen soldier's mother which demanded a full explanation of her son's death. I did not forbid them from writing letters to family members, but I emphasized that they must be mindful of language that suggested incompetence or complacency on the part of anyone in the medical chain unless there was credible evidence to support such claims. I also emphasized that not everyone saw the medic crawling under enemy fire to reach the corporal as I did.

The grieving mother wrote one more letter to me, but I was not allowed to respond. I was deeply saddened by such rigid rules. I suppose that that lesson was part of my education as a young officer and commander of troops.

XIV

Rushing Waters

It was December 1968 and I had been in command of a rifle company in the delta region of South Vietnam for a little more than two months. We were on a reconnaissance in force mission. Our assignment was to sweep through several kilometers of terrain to ensure that enemy forces were not present, then ambush a major canal and its tributaries overnight. Although the area was new to me, several of my men were familiar with it.

Since these canals were such a constant factor in our operating environment, they deserve special explanation at this point. Beginning in 1867, the French colonized three provinces of the southwest region of Vietnam and invested in the digging and expanding of canals and creeks. History books claim that their decision to make such an investment was largely for selfish reasons, but such initiatives ultimately worked to the great economic benefit of the rice farmers. The Viet Minh forced the French to withdraw from Vietnam after they defeated the Europeans in 1954. The waterways that remained were useful for general transportation and commerce. They were likewise useful to the VC for transporting heavy weapons, logistical supplies, and personnel to otherwise inaccessible places in our area of operation. Since the waterways flowed into the great Mekong River near its confluence with the Pacific Ocean, they were affected by the ocean tidal action; thus, they rushed with very strong currents at times and their depths changed appreciably. Adding to their hazardous characteristics was the accumulation of deep, soft mud along their banks and bottoms. This mud was a serious hazard that was unforgiving, resulting in the drowning of a soldier in a sister unit.

Except for the monotony of walking through rice paddies, that morning had been uneventful. We found some booby traps but

XIV. Rushing Waters

fortunately were not injured by them. We simply exploded them in place in accordance with my policy.

Slightly past midmorning, we arrived at the big canal that was between us and our ambush site. I immediately ordered the second and third platoons to place men at least 100 yards on the left and right, respectively, for security. The mortar platoon secured our rear while the first platoon prepared to assist in crossing the canal. The water was deep and flowing very swiftly toward the great river. My RTOs and I settled into a cluster of trees for protection from snipers.

One of the men of the first platoon appeared with a long rope which he tied through his belt in the back of his pants. He and another man removed their boots and fatigue shirts, walked to the edge of the canal and dove into the muddy, fast-flowing water. They were obviously good swimmers but were taken by the strong current as they swam for the distant bank. They reached the opposite side of the canal and, after making their way laboriously through the deep mud, climbed onto the opposite bank. They turned toward the closest large tree, planning to tie the rope to it. However, their routine was interrupted by shouts from my side of the canal.

The unexpected commotion started when a young soldier of the first platoon walked to the canal bank near us. He was shirtless but still wore his boots. Once at the bank's edge, he bellowed what sounded like a rebel yell and dove into the water. It was evident immediately that he was headed for trouble because he was making very little headway toward the opposite bank and the current was sweeping him downstream at great speed. He began quickly to yell for help. One of the good swimmers on the opposite bank ran toward the distressed soldier and dived into the canal near him. Before he could reach him, however, the struggling soldier was pulled under by the current.

Then, to heighten my level of anxiety, the rescuing swimmer went underwater. However, his disappearance into the muddy water appeared to be deliberate. When he did not resurface right away, I instructed the first platoon leader to get some more men ready with a rope to run down the canal and rescue what now appeared to be two men in distress. I was determined that these soldiers would not die in this manner. Suddenly, the good swimmer surfaced, coughed a couple of times, and began swimming to the canal bank—pulling the drowning soldier with one arm cradled around his neck. As soon as

Part 2—When Things Go Wrong in Combat

he was able to drag the drowning man to solid ground, he placed him on his stomach and began pressing his rib cage. The other soldier, who swam the canal with the rescuer, joined him and began pressing the water out of the stricken soldier's lungs. Then they turned him onto his back and began mouth-to-mouth resuscitation. I nearly wept with joy when I saw the soldier begin to move around and cough. I felt a calm sweep over me at that point, and I looked skyward and whispered my gratitude.

One of the swimmers remained with the unwise and unlucky soldier while the other tied one end of the long rope to a large tree. Then he walked a short distance to a cluster of peasant hooches and borrowed one of their sampans. By the time he paddled upstream to our crossing point, the rope was tautly secured on the near bank and ready to use in ferrying ourselves across the canal.

The sampan could accommodate only four men each trip, so the platoon medic and my senior medic were among the first to cross. Fortunately, the crossing went smoothly after everything was set up and operating.

As soon as my RTOs and I crossed, the senior medic approached me and recommended that the resuscitated soldier be evacuated. I concurred and immediately ordered a medevac. Once calm again prevailed, I walked to the area where the medics were still attending the young soldier. I asked him why he had done such a foolish and risky thing. Before he could answer, I reminded him that he had potentially placed us at greater risk of snipers because we had spent much too long in that area and were totally distracted from our mission by his actions. I also reminded him that he was rescued by a man who risked his own life in the process. He looked away from me and said, "I don't know, sir. I felt that I should be the one swimming to the other side, so I just dove in. I just underestimated the strength of the water." I told him that I did not expect him to be evacuated beyond the evac hospital in our division base camp. Therefore, I anticipated his return to our unit to become one of my best soldiers, and if he ever pulled a stunt like that again, I would have him court-martialed. I then wished him well and a complete recovery.

When we returned to the rear area three days later, I visited the hospital. The staff told me that the young soldier was hospitalized for two nights and part of three days while they kept him under observation and administered antibiotics. They explained that there was

XIV. Rushing Waters

great potential for the onset of pneumonia from the polluted water as well as the possibility for him to suffer serious intestinal issues from swallowing the water.

He ultimately became one of my best soldiers. Sadly, I must end this story by reporting that he was wounded about two months later by fragmentation from a booby trap that was tripped by another soldier. The incident occurred during a night operation, so I did not get to see him before he was loaded onto a medevac chopper. His wounds were such that he was evacuated out of Vietnam, so he did not return to our unit and I never knew his fate.

XV

Careless Enemy

It was late morning one day in the last week of January 1969. By this time, I had been in command of a rifle company for three months in the Mekong Delta some 60 miles south of Saigon. This was our second day for sustained operations in an area that was familiar to us because we had been dispatched to it multiple times. Much of the time, we were sent into the area during daylight hours, which naturally gave the local VC guerrillas plenty of time to warn their comrades, set booby traps on trails, and on occasion, fire small mortar rounds or automatic weapons at us. We rarely were able to exact our revenge on the elusive enemy.

During this particular operation, we had ambushed canals in the area day and night, therein denying the waterways to the enemy. During the previous night, I received instructions to ambush a larger canal that was about three kilometers east of us. After establishing an agenda and estimating timelines for the day, I called my platoon leaders and senior NCOs together and explained that I wanted the company to move stealthily through the wooded area to a target that I had in mind. We knew that the local guerrillas frequently used two thatched hooches near a wooded area that was between us and our next ambush site. In previous engagements with them, they managed to fire AK rounds or mortars at us from the vicinity of the hooches and vanish to their hiding places as we pursued them.

I emphasized that we must move quietly, minimize conversation, and secure all rifle slings and other equipment that could produce a noise. I also ordered that no one was to break out of the wood line into the cleared area and that if we encountered any noncombatants, they were to be detained and forced to accompany us until we engaged the targeted area. Since we were still near two canals, I issued a caution regarding walking near them. The two hooches were

XV. Careless Enemy

about a kilometer from us and were situated about 50 meters from the edge of the wood line.

After about half an hour, I received a heads-up from all four platoons. We moved out with the third platoon on point. Fate would not smile on us for the first part of our mission because two of my men walked so close to a canal that they were exposed and shot with automatic weapons fire from the opposite side. Naturally, this constituted an emergency that required immediate action. Fortunately, we found a cleared area not far from our location where we could bring in a medevac. Bringing in a helicopter so close to our target dashed my hopes of any element of surprise. The process of locating a suitable LZ and securing it for the medevac consumed about a half hour. After the helicopter lifted off with the wounded soldiers, I calmed down and decided that we would proceed with the stealth mission despite the delay and calamitous results.

I was very pleased with the movement of my unit of nearly 100 men through wooded and uneven terrain because I hardly heard a sound for the remainder of the trek to the target. After about 25 minutes, I got a call from my third platoon leader.

"Charlie Six, this is Charlie Three," the lieutenant whispered into the radio's handset.

"Roger. This is Six, over."

"I can see the smaller of the two hooches. I don't see any movement, but smoke is rising from the smaller hooch. I'll hold fast until everyone catches up to us, over."

"Roger. Don't engage, even if you see VC, unless you're convinced that they've spotted you. I'll bring up the rest of the company and we'll all get on line before we engage."

"Roger. Willco."

I ordered everyone on line—even the men of the mortar platoon and my CP group. I wanted everyone to participate because what we were about to do was something most soldiers loved to do—provided the end result was favorable.

Once I was convinced that everyone was in place, I spoke over my radio to the platoon leaders: "In three minutes, everyone is to begin firing his weapon at both hooches."

I studied my watch as the second hand moved ahead 180 times. At that point, I raised my M-16 rifle and began firing at the small hooch. The din was deafening because the M-79 grenadiers were

Part 2—When Things Go Wrong in Combat

firing 40 mm grenades at the hooch and the M-60 gunners sent tracers through both hooches. As I fired semiautomatic rounds into the small thatched structure, I assumed that it was vacant because there was no movement to convince me that it was occupied. Suddenly, I spotted a VC fleeing from the small hooch. He was running behind a rice paddy dike with only the top of his head and a small portion of his back exposed. I continued to fire rounds until I saw him fall. After several more minutes, I called a ceasefire and sent the third platoon to clear the two hooches and check for booby traps. After about 20 minutes, the third platoon leader gave me a thumbs-up.

My two radio operators and I walked directly to the spot where I had engaged the enemy soldier. I had my M-16 rifle at the ready because I thought he might still be alive; however, he was not where I expected to find him. In fact, he had escaped completely, leaving a significant blood trail. We had killed two enemy combatants, and the third platoon leader reported that he saw two others escaping, so we knew that at least five VC had been in the hooch when we engaged it. I was disappointed that we had not killed all of the enemy combatants. However, I must admit that at the same time, I was as jubilant as my soldiers because we had demonstrated to the enemy that he can never relax his guard. For the next two hours, we gloated over our successful mission and engaged in the old adage, "To the victor go the spoils." The small group of VC fighters must have been preparing to cook a meal because we found a flat piece of cast iron over some hot coals with a dented, aluminum pot nearly full of hot water. Some of the men spotted several young chickens. They also found two poles with gigs on the ends that would ordinarily be used for hunting frogs. One of my subordinates, who was a country boy, suggested that the chickens would make a savory meal. After I agreed that we would take the time to cook a couple, the troops began chasing and collecting them with the frog gigs. Several troops, who claimed to have experience at processing chickens, skinned and cut them into smaller pieces so they would cook faster. Others kindled the fire, and within a few minutes, several pieces of chicken were simmering on the flat piece of iron.

In the meantime, I accompanied a small team to the larger hooch to inspect it and ensure that we had not overlooked anything. One of the sergeants called my attention to the large clay pot that stood in one corner. When he lifted the wooden lid, we discovered

XV. Careless Enemy

that it was half full of rice. The little demon, which sits astride my left shoulder, whispered in my ear that the top of the pot was roughly the size of a toilet seat and suggested that pooping in the enemy's rice bowl was the ultimate insult. After some of the men moved the rice bowl to a more discreet location, several of us took advantage of its comforts.

While the chicken was cooking, some troops began shooting the captured AK-47 rifles. No sooner had the firing started than one of my sergeants burst into the hooch and reported that some of the men were using the captured weapons to shoot the remaining chickens. He stated that it was meant to add insult to injury by denying the enemy his food source. After looking outside of the hooch at the mayhem, I called a halt to the shooting for fear that the men might shoot one another.

After about an hour, the first of the blackened pieces of chicken appeared ready to eat. I accepted a wing, poured a substantial amount of hot sauce on it and ate it, giving it a rating of five out of 10. It was not completely cooked near the bone, but I ate it in spite of this shortcoming. I told my platoon leaders that we would spend one more hour in the area before moving closer to our ambush site for the night. Some of the men asked if there would be time to cook another batch of chicken for their friends who were posted around our perimeter on security duty. I readily agreed that they should treat them to the remainder of the chicken.

By 1400 hours, I felt that we should move to within one kilometer of our night ambush site. So I alerted the platoon leaders to collect their men and recall those who were posted on security. We returned to the wooded area where the walking was more difficult but where we could move with greater stealth—denying the prying eyes of the enemy and his local supporters knowledge of our movement. Since we were not using trails, movement was more difficult, especially when crossing several small streams. We finally arrived at some high ground that was dry and within 500 meters of our ambush site. After instructing the platoon leaders to post security all around, I told the second platoon leader to post a small group to our north where they could observe that area until dark. I also instructed the platoon leaders to let as many men as possible rest because typically there was very little sleep or rest during these night ambushes.

I brushed my teeth and found a grassy spot near a small tree. I

Part 2—When Things Go Wrong in Combat

sat on the ground near my two radio operators, leaned against the tree, and closed my eyes. I had not been resting more than a few minutes when I heard the second platoon leader's voice on the company radio.

"Charlie Six, this is Charlie Two, over."

I crawled several feet to my RTOs. As I arrived, the operator on the company net offered me the handset to his radio.

"This is Charlie Six, over."

"My elements just informed me that they spotted a man on the far side of the cleared area to the north. They say he's behaving strangely by hugging the wood line and stopping frequently to check the area behind him. And when a chopper flew over a few minutes ago, he jumped back in the woods and waited for it to fly past him. They also believe he's carrying a rifle. Over."

"Roger. I'll come to your location. I have some binoculars that we can use to verify that he's an enemy combatant."

By this time, both RTOs were watching me, waiting for my signal to move out. I secured my backpack and M-16 rifle and motioned for them to follow. As we walked slowly and cautiously through the dense vegetation, we were met by the second platoon leader.

"My men, who are overlooking the open area, are just a few meters ahead. We're whispering only and staying well clear of the edge of the clearing. That man appears to be very paranoid and alert and might see us if we get too close to the edge. If you don't mind, Sir, leave your two RTOs back here. The fewer bodies up there, the better."

I motioned for my RTOs to remain in place as I dug into my pack for the binoculars. We walked slowly and quietly forward until we met the four men from the second platoon. I greeted them and knelt on the ground near the sergeant in charge of the group. I could see excitement in his eyes as he turned and began to speak.

"You can see him at a distance of about 100 meters, Captain. I think he's a VC," he said as he pointed to his right front.

"Roger, I see him moving just inside the wood line. I'll check him out with my binoculars."

I raised the glasses to my eyes, and a minor adjustment enabled me to see the enemy soldier plainly.

"He's clearly a Viet Cong. He has a VC uniform, an AK rifle, and a small pack on his back. He'll soon come to the end of the clearing.

XV. Careless Enemy

If he turns toward us, let him come to us, but if he continues to walk in the same direction, shoot and kill him. My preference is to capture him because the intel weenies will love a fresh, warm source of information."

The enemy soldier walked tentatively to the end of the clearing and turned in our direction. I held my breath as he reached the point where he could turn to his left and stay near the wood line or continue straight toward us. As he entered the open space between the two wood lines, he quickened his pace.

In the meantime, the second platoon leader had positioned four other soldiers on either side of a small trail nearby. I could see the men but could not see that they were next to a trail.

We watched anxiously with all firearms at the ready as the VC soldier walked toward us, peering nervously in all directions. I watched as he entered the wood line and walked along the trail where four American fighting men awaited his arrival.

Suddenly, one of the soldiers jumped from the brush and grabbed the unsuspecting VC. He was able to trap him because he was able to reach completely around the smaller man's body. A second soldier leaped forward and grabbed the AK-47 rifle from the VC's grasp.

Once the enemy was disarmed, the soldier released his grip. As I walked toward the trail, I watched the young captive. As soon as he was released, he spun around nervously to find himself encircled by U.S. infantrymen. Apparently, he realized intuitively that if he tried to run, he would be killed.

Upon reaching the group, I slipped through the circle and walked toward the prisoner. Despite the absence of any rank insignia on my jungle fatigues, the young VC must have sensed that I was an authority figure. His eyes grew larger and he began to back away from me. I could see great fear and panic in his eyes. He was breathing rapidly and the veins bulged in his neck.

I followed close to him, shouting, "You little son of a bitch, you were in that hooch, weren't you? It was you who seeded the trails with booby traps and punji stakes. You probably enjoyed firing mortars at us, didn't you? You managed to escape, but you walked directly into our hands. Now the shoe is on the other foot." Instinctively, I slapped him and sent him reeling backward as an act of revenge for all the booby traps that had injured and maimed my fellow soldiers in that

Part 2—When Things Go Wrong in Combat

area. I caught myself before inflicting any more harm on this small, young Vietnamese man. I was embarrassed that my soldiers had seen me commit an act that I had admonished them for doing.

The men gloated at how Corporal Long had simply jumped out and grabbed the unsuspecting enemy. We also inspected the contents of his pack, finding only a set of black "pajamas" and a small map with some lines and symbols on it.

I reluctantly notified battalion operations that we had captured a VC prisoner and gave them all the known details of the capture. Not much time passed before I received a request from the battalion intelligence officer to secure an open area nearby so that a small helicopter could transport the prisoner to the forward support base for interrogation. Of course, I disapproved of this course of action because it alerted the enemy in the area to our presence. In fact, it could spoil our plans for executing an ambush within a kilometer of our current location or give the local VC cells the time and opportunity to plant booby traps along the major routes in both directions.

As soon as the light observation helicopter lifted off the ground with the prisoner, I called my platoon leaders to my location for a coordination meeting. I told them that I wanted to stay inside the wood line and move about 500 meters from our present location.

"Once we've moved, let's put out listening posts of four men each on major trails. About 30 minutes after dark, we'll move the remaining distance to our ambush site. In the meantime, tell your men that if they want to heat food, do it during daylight hours. Any questions?"

We succeeded in traveling the remaining distance to our ambush site without incident, and the night was dull and uneventful. The local VC guerrillas had ample time to warn all of their followers and supporters of our presence, what with our attack on the hooches and the arrival of the helicopter to retrieve one of their own. However, I was firmly convinced that we had instilled a level of fear and dread in the hearts of the enemy survivors that was unprecedented. As I told my troops in a unit formation a few days later, our behavior was very unorthodox, and it surely frightened the hell out of the enemy.

XVI

The Enemy Celebrates

It was late January 1969 and I had been in command of a rifle company for more than three months. My parent battalion was frequently assigned missions related to securing the Ninth Infantry Division base camp. Accordingly, my company was ordered to sweep an area about 12 kilometers west of the base camp because the enemy had launched 120 mm mortars from this area within the last week. We were transported up the Mekong River by landing craft that were part of the Riverine Force. Once we were delivered to our insertion point, our orders were to conduct a reconnaissance in force for another eight kilometers during daylight and ambush two major canals overnight. The following day, we were to walk out of the area to be picked up by trucks and transported to one of the firebases that provided artillery support within our area of operation.

When I reviewed the mission statement of our order, a couple of factors came to mind. First, we would be required to cross a major canal whose waters were swift and deep. We were old hands at crossing this canal and knew several sources of sampans that we could "borrow" for transporting ourselves across. However, the matter of moving my company to the banks of a major canal and then remaining at or near the canal banks long enough to transport everyone across simply provided an ideal opportunity for the enemy to ambush us. This factor alone made me very nervous. The second factor involved the uncertain availability of artillery support. We might be beyond the range of 105 mm artillery but were within range of 155 mm artillery. I wasn't comfortable with the larger artillery in some circumstances because of its much greater bursting radius. There were times when it was not safe or prudent to bring it as close as was needed to kill or deter the enemy or enable us to break contact from the enemy safely.

Part 2—When Things Go Wrong in Combat

After completing the insertion, I deployed the company with the three rifle platoons abreast and the mortar platoon providing rear security. We covered a swath roughly two football fields wide. We made our way to the big canal and crossed it without incident. Then we covered the last few kilometers in time to arrive just before twilight. In keeping with my policy, we did not move into our ambush positions until after dark.

The targeted area consisted of two canals: a small canal that flowed east-west and spilled into the larger one that flowed north-south. In the briefing that I received for this mission, the battalion intelligence officer stated that the enemy was using the waterways in this remote area to transport heavy weapons and troops into our area of operation.

I placed two rifle platoons in ambush positions on the larger canal and the third rifle platoon on the smaller one. The mortar platoon was assigned the mission of rear security. The first several hours of the night passed without incident; however, at 0230 hours, both rifle platoons on the larger canal began firing. They absolutely lit the night sky with fire from M-60 machine guns, M-79 grenade launchers, and M-16 rifles. I grinned because I knew that the troops relished such a fight. The enemy was able to fire a few rounds in return before the firing ceased. I could hear excited voices in the second platoon yelling back and forth, then I heard a very distinct voice yelling, "Chieu Hoi." This phrase was a call to surrender in Vietnamese. I immediately called the second platoon on the radio and advised the platoon leader to stay alert in case a larger force might be following these sampans. After he acknowledged my instructions, I made my way to the first platoon. I did not press the platoon leader for information until I was certain that everything was under control. Actually, he and his platoon sergeant approached me and began to relate the details of the engagement.

"Sir, we know that there were five sampans. Of course, the first platoon didn't discover this small convoy until two large sampans had gone past them. They opened fire on the last three; then my men were alerted in time to engage the remaining two as they tried to sneak past us. Both sampans appeared to carry heavy cargo because they sunk very fast. As far as we can tell, only one enemy survived. He's wounded in his right leg, but my medic says that his wound is not life threatening."

XVI. The Enemy Celebrates

"Thanks for the update. I'm very proud of you and your men. Was anyone hit with the few rounds that they fired at us, and are you sure that everything went to the bottom of the large canal?"

"In answering your first question: no, Sir, no one was hit by the incoming fire. My men popped a handheld flare as soon as the firing started, and it illuminated the canal and the sampans very well. The M-60 gunners destroyed the sampans—filling them full of big holes. They went down very fast, and the kill zone was illuminated so well that the enemy soldiers were sitting ducks. In fact, the one VC who survived is a very lucky man," the lieutenant stated matter-of-factly.

"As for the POW, make sure that your men don't torture him. It's OK with me if you hog-tie him for the rest of the night. We'll get rid of him tomorrow when we reach the firebase and turn him over to the intel weenies or the military police."

After ensuring that everything was under control in the second platoon area, I made my way to the first platoon. After meeting the acting platoon leader, a staff sergeant, he briefed me on their actions.

"My men spotted three sampans in time to engage them and sink them in the swift waters of the canal. We didn't realize that two sampans had already passed our kill zone until the second platoon began firing on them. I know that my men were not asleep because I was sitting near them having a cup of coffee. I'm sure that you know that enemy fighters are disciplined when they travel these waterways. They're masters at paddling the sampans quietly, and they use hand signals to communicate, so there is very little noise. We usually detect them by sight only. The second platoon leader called just before you arrived and told me that his men sunk the other two sampans and that they captured one VC. I would say that this has been a productive operation because those sampans appeared to be loaded with heavy objects."

I jotted down a few cryptic lines and handed them to my radio operator to report to the battalion operations center. Naturally, there was immediate interest in the POW. I merely explained that we would deliver him later that day. After all, it was already 0330 hours, and we planned to depart this area within a couple of hours.

It was very difficult to sleep after such an engagement because adrenaline was still in my system. I didn't bother to lie down again; instead, I sat next to a tree and leaned against it. I think I may have dozed but finally gave up on sleeping at daylight. We departed the

Part 2—When Things Go Wrong in Combat

ambush site at a little past 0600 hours. We took the same route back, which had us crossing the big, dreaded canal at the same point we had used the previous day. This particular crossing point was one of the few that was near peasant hooches where we could "borrow" a couple of sampans.

When we drew within one kilometer of the crossing point, I ordered a halt and instructed everyone to take a break, drink some water, and eat something if they wished. I also told them that there would not be another good chance for a food break until we closed on the firebase later in the day. I heated water in my canteen cup and made instant C-ration coffee. Before I sat by a tree and leaned against it, I motioned for my artillery forward observer to come and sit near me. He possessed exceptional skill at placing "calls for fire" and adjusting the rounds when they were needed.

"Dan, after we make our way across this big canal, I'd like for you to call your battalion fire direction officer and determine if we can order a few rounds of high-explosive 155 mm rounds to be fired on the site that we just left. I'm certain that the VC will come and investigate the area within several hours. Some of their elements had to hear the engagement this morning, and they will surely come to investigate. Let's treat them to an early Fourth of July celebration," I explained as I opened a can of C-ration ham and lima beans.

The lieutenant took notes the entire time I was talking. When I finished, he jammed his notepad in his pocket and said, "Got it, Sir. I'll let you know if we can pull this off."

After about 30 minutes, we continued our trek in the direction of the big canal. The canals in the Mekong Delta were affected by the tide, some more than others. We were not very far from the confluence of the Mekong River into the South China Sea, so the tidal effects in our area of operation could be very strong.

When we arrived, the tide was obviously going out because the water was flowing south very swiftly. I halted the company and called all four platoon leaders to my location to brief them on my plan.

"First platoon, you're to take the center and prepare the means for ferrying the company to the other side. As we've done before, send two men down to the peasant hooches and borrow a couple of sampans. Paddle them up here, then have one of the men paddle a sampan across with one end of the rope. Once the rope has been secured to stationary objects on both banks, transport the remainder of your

XVI. The Enemy Celebrates

platoon to the other side. Once you have accomplished the crossing, place men north and south at least 100 meters in each direction. Second platoon, post at least a squad 100 meters to our south to protect our right flank. Also, you are to be the last to cross because I'm concerned about snipers from the south. Third platoon, position at least a squad about 100 meters north in order to protect our left flank. Mortar platoon, secure our rear, and you are to be the second to cross. When you get to the other side, set up a mortar just in case we need it. My CP group and I will follow the mortar platoon. Third platoon follows us. Any questions?"

I motioned for my radio operators to follow as I moved close enough to the canal to observe the process. Within about 10 minutes, the four troops arrived with the "borrowed" sampans. Corporal Brauer, who was in the front of the leading sampan, took the end of the rope. Then he and his companion began paddling very hard through the swift water to the other side. I observed that the corporal was a young soldier from Kentucky. He had impressed me several times with his can-do attitude and natural leadership skills. In fact, he was one of the volunteers who swam across the canal with the rope when we crossed the previous day. After securing the rope to a sizable tree on the opposite side of the canal and pulling it as tight as possible, the corporal remained on the edge of the canal while his companion pulled himself and the sampan back to our side. The mud was a complicating factor on both sides of the river, so the matter of getting into and out of the sampan was tedious. Three men from the first platoon entered one of the sampans and sat down. The man who would draw the sampan across the canal remained standing and began pulling against the strong current. As soon as the first sampan was several feet from the bank, the second sampan began to receive its passengers. Corporal Brauer was standing in the mud on the opposite side, waiting to assist passengers in stepping out of the sampan and negotiating the deep mud to solid ground farther up the bank. It was a tedious, slow, and dangerous process.

Both the first platoon and the mortar platoon crossed without incident. My radio operators and I made our way through the mud and sat in one of the sampans to be pulled across the canal. When we reached the opposite side, Corporal Brauer met us at water's edge. He reached for my hand as he did for everyone else trying to step from the shaky sampan. After steadying me, he pulled gently on my hand

Part 2—When Things Go Wrong in Combat

and continued to aid me in negotiating the deep mud until we were close to the bank. I stood upright for a moment, made eye contact with him, and said, "Corporal, you're doing a great job. Thanks for the help." As I took the next step, I heard the all-too-familiar crack of a bullet. The young corporal fell in a heap next to me. I know I must have grown pale, realizing that had I not taken the step, the bullet could have hit me. Since the crack of the rifle came from the south, I moved quickly to a tree that was between the shooter and me. It was typical for snipers to target radio operators and men near them. Their primary targets, however, were officers, senior NCOs, and radio operators.

Men from the first platoon quickly began to fire in the direction of the sound. The first platoon leader called to notify me that the shooter was at least 100 meters south of his men and across the small canal that flowed into the large one. He also said that his men were unable to spot the shooter. That bit of information indicated that the shooter's location was between 250 and 300 meters from Corporal Brauer.

It was foolhardy to think that we could go after the shooter. He had thoroughly planned and executed his attack. Placing himself on the opposite side of yet another canal from us more or less ensured an easy escape.

I transmitted instructions to the mortar platoon leader to bring the 60 mm mortar to my location. As I waited for him, the mortar platoon medic approached and informed me that Corporal Brauer had been killed instantly by the sniper's bullet. I moved closer to my radio operator and told him to request a medevac. As I waited for the mortar platoon leader to arrive, I felt the familiar sadness creeping into my thoughts. I simply had no time to mourn the loss of this amazing young soldier. That would have to wait, but I could not escape the anger, fear, and dread that continued their attempts to overshadow rational thinking. I was familiar with the enemy's methods, and I knew that the sniper likely fled the area as soon as his shot was delivered. Therefore, there was little likelihood that he would be foolish enough to make further attempts at sniping at us. However, I couldn't accept the risk that he was still present and motivated to kill more of us.

Within five minutes, the mortar platoon sergeant and five others arrived carrying the mortar tube with accessories and several rounds

XVI. The Enemy Celebrates

of 60 mm ammunition. I instructed him to join the men of the first platoon who had fired shots in the direction of the sniper. I opined that they should know the approximate distance and direction of the shooter. I instructed him to fire a couple of rounds into the probable location of the shooter and continue to fire a round or two every 10 minutes until we were ready to leave.

Some of the men from the mortar platoon made an improvised litter with which to transport Corporal Brauer to the LZ and load him onto the medevac. After the medevac mission was completed and we succeeded in transporting the remainder of the company across the big canal, I ordered everyone to prepare to move out. The sniper incident had delayed our movement by at least an hour and a half.

The remainder of our trek to the firebase was uneventful. My company replaced a sister company of our battalion as the security force for the firebase. The next day, I briefed the battalion operations officer and the battalion commander on my company's activities for the past two days. Afterward, I requested that all of the platoon leaders and platoon sergeants come to the bunker where I had set up my CP. After they arrived, I spoke about the last operation.

"Two nights ago, we met with great success against the enemy. We sunk five enemy sampans that were heavily loaded, giving us every reason to thump our chests. We also killed at least nine of their fighters in our ambushes and took one of their members prisoner—again, giving us reason to beat our chests like lowland silverback gorillas. Then yesterday, the enemy succeeded in killing one of us despite our security measures. While we mourn the loss of our fellow American, the sniper probably pumped his fist in the air and carved another notch on his rifle stock. Please inform your men that the chaplain told me that he will conduct a memorial service the next time we have a stand-down in the division base camp. That will be a time for us to honor Corporal Brauer. He was one of our finest. By the way, the battalion intelligence officer informed me that when the POW was interrogated, he revealed that 12 men had been on the five sampans. He also stated that they were transporting two 120 mm mortars with 200 rounds of ammunition, five 122 mm Katyusha rockets, and assorted small arms ammunition. The battalion commander agrees that 155 mm artillery rounds should be fired on the scene of our ambush. With his support, I'm confident that it will happen. So maybe, just maybe, we will still have the last word."

XVII

Fateful Night Mission

It was late February 1969 and I was commanding a rifle company in the Sixth Battalion, 31st Infantry Regiment, Ninth Infantry Division in the Mekong Delta of South Vietnam. My company had been engaged in air assault missions for nearly two days, with overnight ambushes on major canals, when I received an unsettling message from the battalion operations officer. Instead of being picked up by helicopters for transport to the Ninth Infantry Division base camp for a stand-down, we were to trek during the night to a large village. Our order stated that we were to constitute a significant part of a cordon that required us to be in place before daylight the following morning and link up with Regional Force (RF) and Popular Force (PF).*

Much of the area between our present location and the targeted area was familiar to us, but moving long distances at night without the benefit of light sources presented many and varied challenges. The only time I dared position flank security during night movements was when moving through rice paddies; otherwise, we traveled in single file. Wooded areas usually contained paths that were used frequently by locals. Such paths were preferred by the locals because they constituted the easiest way to negotiate the difficult terrain. The VC recognized these features and frequently placed booby traps on them to deny usage by their enemies.

I halted movement and instructed everyone to take a break, encouraging them to eat and rest for a half hour. I also asked my platoon leaders and their senior sergeants to come to my location. I immediately opened C-ration cans and started heating a can of ham and lima beans. After my subordinates arrived, I encouraged them to eat as I ate my own food and briefed them on the new mission.

---

*RFs/PFs were the equivalent of militias. They were usually deployed in their own regions to protect local communities.

XVII. Fateful Night Mission

"Men, we have a change of mission. Given my behavior over the last half hour, you probably sensed that something is amiss. We'll travel overnight to a large village that we've passed many times. It's near Highway 4, slightly more than five kilometers from here. First platoon, you'll take the lead. We can chance walking on trails because the VC won't know that we're moving near or through their area unless we're forced to fire our weapons or call in a medevac. First platoon, you're to post flank security in open rice paddies only. In wooded areas, we have no choice but to walk in file formation. We have to arrive at the designated site in time to link up with RFs and PFs before dawn. Experience teaches me that linking up with such forces is never quick and easy. Communications are always a problem, and we must be extra cautious because we'll be approaching their area during darkness. We've all moved at night, so we know how tedious and tiring it can be. If we can travel at a speed of three-quarters of a kilometer per hour, we should arrive in plenty of time. I know everyone is tired. We've been on the move for two days, and we slept very little last night. If we're lucky, maybe we can reach our target early enough to get a little rest before the search of the village begins after daylight. Any questions?"

There were no questions, so I dismissed everyone except the first platoon leader. He and I studied the map together and settled on the azimuth that we should follow to avoid any peasant villages along the way and to reach the target.

The first kilometer went pretty smoothly with us making good time. We walked through open terrain with lots of rice paddies. Some of them were dry—giving us good footing and easy movement. The next two kilometers were wooded and presented more difficult challenges because there were occasional streams to cross. After we were nearly a kilometer into the wooded zone, the first platoon leader found a trail that ran close to our direction of travel. We began to cross one of the pole bridges that was put in place by the locals for crossing small streams.

My regular senior medic was away on a well-deserved R and R trip. The medic, who showed up as his temporary replacement, was overweight. I suspected that either he had never been assigned as a combat medic or that he had not served as one long enough to shed the extra weight. His movement was unusually slow in the wet, muddy rice paddies, and he was clumsy when crossing the streams.

Part 2—When Things Go Wrong in Combat

We came to a stream after midnight that was wider than most but had a pole bridge spanning its width. It had a crude handrail, but sections of it were missing, causing us to walk several feet occasionally with no support. I heard two men of the first platoon fall from the poles into the waist-deep water. When they were helped back to the poles, water dripped from their clothing—making the surfaces slippery. I determined later that both men had slipped off the left side of the crude bridge.

My CP group consisted of my two radio operators, the artillery forward observer (FO) and his radio operator, the replacement senior medic, and me. As we approached the bridge, one of my radio operators notified me that the battery on his radio was dying, so I told the FO and his radio operator and the senior medic to pass us and cross the bridge. I happened to see the medic when he approached a gap in the handrails. Despite the assistance he was getting from the FO's radio operator, he slipped from the poles and fell into the water on the right side of the bridge. He immediately began screaming for help. Fearing the worst, I viewed both sides of the bridge as ideal places for the enemy to drive punji stakes into the bottom—where they would wait silently for some hapless victim.

The second platoon followed my CP group in the long procession, so I asked the platoon leader to send two men to extricate the injured medic from the punji pit. I also asked him to send his platoon medic forward to treat and evaluate the wounded man. The senior medic was shouting, "A punji is stuck in the calf of my left leg and I can't pull it out."

When the two men arrived from the second platoon, I called them aside and issued some instructions. "I'll tell the medic that he has to try harder to pull himself free from the punji. If he tries harder but fails, then one of you go in and help to free him and bring him out of the water. There is a real danger that there are more punji stakes or possibly a booby-trapped explosive device. If he can pull free of the punji, then toss him a rope and pull him to safety."

After the two men acknowledged my instructions, I turned and yelled to the medic to try harder to free himself from the punji. In the meantime, one of the men walked along the pole bridge nearly to the place where the medic slipped and fell. He tossed one end of the rope to him and told him that he was going back to the bank so he would have firm footing for pulling. Soon the medic shouted that

XVII. Fateful Night Mission

the punji was finally out of his leg but that he was stuck in the muddy bottom. The two men pulled on the rope and soon drew the medic near the edge of the stream. Then they grabbed him under his arms and pulled him out of the water onto the grassy edge.

The second platoon medic took over immediately. His first action was to give the wounded man a morphine injection. Then he began cutting off his pant leg above the knee. He looked up at the two men from the second platoon and said, "Hold him. I'm going to clean his wound and examine it. It's not going to be pretty or painless." Waiting until the two men were holding the injured man firmly under his arms, he began pouring cleansing liquids on the wound and examining it. Lots of blood poured from the wound, convincing me that a medevac was required.

I could see from the details of my map that there was a cleared area ahead about 100 meters. I instructed the first platoon, whose men were already across the stream, to continue to the clearing and secure an open area big enough for the medevac to land. The wounded man was unable to walk, so we had to carry him on an improvised stretcher. This forced the litter bearers to walk through two bodies of water instead of crossing on the pole bridges. I held my breath each time for fear of more punji stakes. We spent more than an hour completing the evacuation—time we could ill afford. The men from the first platoon cut a sapling and tied their strobe light onto the end of it. This process was the safest means to enable the chopper pilot to locate the cleared area. Another inevitable result of our activities was the disclosure of our presence to the local VC guerrillas.

By the time the remainder of my company cleared the wooded area and all of its obstacles, it was 0145 hours. We had surely fallen behind, so I urged the first platoon leader to try and walk faster. Having traveled through some of the terrain previously, I knew that we had rice paddies most of the way to the target. We moved the next hour and a half without incident.

The air was heavy with high humidity, and there was an eerie quiet that prevailed as we plodded along one foot in front of the other. I suddenly realized that we were traveling on an old trail that was about four feet wide and felt firm under our feet. Then a dose of reality jarred me fully alert. My first platoon leader had walked past a fortified RF compound, and my CP group was approaching it. It

Part 2—When Things Go Wrong in Combat

was too late to turn around and it was much too quiet for me to issue a warning over my radio. I thought, "Dear God, let us get past this place without incident."

God must not have heard my plea because the RF sentry on duty fired a shot into the air. Those of us who had experienced operations with or near RFs/PFs knew that this was standard practice. However, a new machine gunner behind us in the second platoon opened fire in the general direction of the shot. The RFs did not return fire, but instincts compelled us to seek cover. That decision proved to be disastrous! Everyone in my CP group scrambled into the shallow ditch opposite the camp. Several of the men of the second platoon who had followed us all night scrambled in behind us. As soon as they entered the ditch behind us, there were several explosions that were followed by the call for a medic. I cringed for fear that the next blast would be caused by a member of my own CP group.

I interpreted the explosions to be the blasts of the dreaded Claymore mines, which were frequently used by U.S. forces in defensive positions. Such mines had been made available to the ARVN and a few were in the hands of the RF/PF.

I began yelling, "Cease fire" and "We're Americans." Desperate to prevent any more casualties or any further exchange of fire, I even took the red lens from my flashlight, put the light under my chin and shone it on my face so that the RF commander could see that we were Americans. I yelled again toward the camp, "Don't fire anymore Claymores." A Vietnamese voice from inside the camp shouted back, "Vietnamese no shoot Claymore." I interpreted that to mean that the explosions were probably booby-trapped hand grenades. I turned and yelled to my CP group and everyone else within range of my voice, "Crawl directly out of the ditch onto the trail. Don't walk in the trail. There may be more booby traps."

I could hear my second platoon leader calling me on the radio handset. I waited for my radio operator to clear the ditch before approaching him.

"This is Charlie Six, over."

"Roger. I have three wounded. Two are serious and one is minor. We need a medevac, over."

"Roger. I'll request one right away. We just passed a cleared area about 60 meters behind us. I'll tell the third platoon to secure it for the chopper. Do you need help carrying the wounded to the pickup, over?"

XVII. Fateful Night Mission

"Negative. My medic needs the supplies from the senior medic's kit, though. I understand that he left it with one of your radio operators. He also needs help from another medic if you could send us one."

"Roger. I'll ask the third platoon to send their medic."

This was not a time for self-doubt, although I blamed myself to a degree for getting us into this chaotic debacle.

By the time we completed all actions relating to the medevac, I was most anxious about reaching the target within our deadline. We moved as fast as possible to travel the remaining half kilometer. As soon as we reached the east side of Highway 4, my radio operator changed his radio to the frequency we were given for the American adviser with the RF/PF. We called repeatedly for more than half an hour before he finally answered.

"This is Tiger 43. Where have you been? We should have been linked up 30 minutes ago, over."

"This is Charlie Six. Why haven't you been monitoring your radio? We've tried for half an hour to raise you. I'm not sending my troops across Highway 4 until I know that your forces are expecting us. So give me the assurances that I need to cross the highway and link up with the RF/PF. My company is spread in the tree line along Highway 4 south of the abandoned hooch, over."

"Roger. One of the RF commanders and I will fire a handheld flare as a signal for you to cross to the west side of the highway. We need you to space your men about every five to ten meters apart to seal the east side of this big village. All the RF and PF will be moving into position at the same time, over."

At twilight, I saw the flare shoot into the sky, so I issued the order to move to the west side of the highway. I had already discussed strategy with the first, second, and third platoons. I told the mortar platoon to set up a mortar and be ready to use it because I didn't know what to expect from the enemy.

I began to feel better about the linkup when my first platoon leader reported that he had spotted RF troops on the other side of a reed-infested stream. The element of surprise was evident by the amount of shooting that occurred inside the village and west of it. There was little activity on our side of the village until about 0830 hours. The first platoon was the first to begin shooting at VC fighters who must have thought that they could sneak through our lines.

Part 2—When Things Go Wrong in Combat

The commander of a Regional Force camp, which protected the village shown in the photograph on the next page. March–April 1969.

Troops of the first platoon shot and killed two. Soon afterward, the third platoon began firing, and they reported killing three.

Two command and control helicopters appeared and began circling the village. I knew that one was my battalion commander, but I did not know who was in the other chopper until I suddenly heard the call sign of the brigade commander on my company frequency.

"Charlie Six, this is Rhinestone Six, over."

"Roger, Rhinestone Six. This is Charlie Six, over."

"This is Rhinestone Six. There is a reed-filled stream just north of one of your elements. The RF have mysteriously moved away and are no longer linked up with your element. When I flew over the stream just now, I saw a VC in the stream underwater. He's floating on his back and breathing through a reed. Send some of your elements to prevent him from getting past you. I'll have the pilot fly over the VC at pretty low level so you can see where he is located, over."

"This is Charlie Six. Roger. I'll send one of my elements down there right away."

XVII. Fateful Night Mission

A Regional Force camp astride Highway 4. This highway was one of the few major highways that facilitated land travel in the Mekong region. My company drew highway-protection duty periodically, and occasionally I set up my command post near the Regional Force camp which facilitated personal relationships with the camp leadership. The road was constructed during the French occupation which ended in 1954.

I watched as the chopper circled around and descended to an altitude of maybe 100 feet. As it flew over the stream, I heard automatic AK fire. Then the brigade commander was on the radio again.

"Charlie Six, this is Rhinestone Six. The chopper took some rounds in the transmission, and I took a round in my hip. We're autorotating to the ground as I speak."

"This is Charlie Six. Roger. Do you need my unit to secure you and the chopper crew? Over."

"This is Rhinestone Six. Negative. Help is already on the way from our base camp. Besides, we're already a mile from your location."

I redirected my attention to the task he had assigned. I called the mortar platoon leader and asked him to come to my location. When he arrived, I told him to take enough men to have a radio, an M-60 machine gun, two riflemen, and a medic and go after the VC who had

Part 2—When Things Go Wrong in Combat

shot the chopper. He was ready to go within five minutes and was all smiles when he passed by my CP with the assembled group.

I did not hear anything from the mortar platoon leader for 15–20 minutes. He finally gave me a situation report (SITREP), telling me that they had reached the stream and were beginning to search up and down it for the enemy.

Suddenly, I heard an M-16 fire one shot; then the M-60 began firing. That was followed by an explosion. I learned later that one of the men took an M-79 grenade launcher with him. Soon after the shooting stopped, the platoon leader reported that they had killed two enemy fighters and captured their AK-47 rifles.

We remained in position for another half hour before I was contacted by the American adviser. First, he requested to know how many of the enemy we had engaged and whether we had captured enemy equipment or weapons. I gave him the count of eight enemy fighters killed and that we had captured seven AK-47 rifles. He stated that we should turn over the rifles to him. I refused emphatically.

I called my platoon leaders on the radio and informed them that we would reassemble about 150 meters south of the village on the east side of the highway for pickup by army trucks. I then called the battalion operations center and informed them that the operation was over and that we were ready for pickup. We traveled the short distance to the pickup area and waited for the trucks. As we waited, the second platoon leader called and asked if I would like to have a VC flag. I said yes and asked if he had one. He replied that some of his men had taken one from a backpack that belonged to one of the dead VC. I thanked the two men who presented it to me and asked one of my radio operators to take my photo with it.

By this time, it was 1400 hours. I suddenly realized that I was famished and exhausted. We had not eaten since before we began our fateful trek the previous evening. I took a chocolate bar from my pack and ate it quickly to try and find some energy. I was elated to see the arrival of the large trucks, knowing that the men were just as anxious as me to get to Fire Support Base Moore where we would have access to a shower, hot food, clean clothes, and some well-earned rest. We were not permitted to have the stand-down that we were destined for the previous day. Instead, my company would have the mission of perimeter security around Fire Support Base Moore. It was not a demanding assignment unless the enemy decided to attack. I was

XVII. Fateful Night Mission

anxiously looking forward to three or four hours of sleep. That was my first priority. At least it was until we unloaded from the trucks and I began walking to the sandbagged bunker that would be my fortified operations center for the next two days and nights. Before I reached the bunker, the battalion operations officer informed me that the battalion commander wanted me to join two other company commanders in his office for a special briefing.

When I walked into the battalion commander's office, he greeted me and motioned for me to sit in one of the chairs in front of his desk. I greeted the other two company commanders before I sat. I remember the battalion commander stating that he intended to cover several topics. One of the main ones was the fact the VC were recovering unexploded artillery rounds and command-detonating them.* A unit of a sister battalion had experienced one of these explosions, and it killed or wounded at least 30 men. The next thing I knew, I felt myself impact the floor. My state of exhaustion had such a grip on me that I was unaware that I was going to sleep and falling to the floor. I stood and apologized to my commander. He looked at me with an understanding expression and told me to go and get some sleep. I gladly complied, and after about four hours, I returned to his office and made an apology my first priority. His only words were, "I understand. I've been there." I knew he did because he had served in the infantry in the Korean War. That three-day operation convinced me that the zombie effect controlled me after two nights and three days of sleep deprivation.

---

*The term "command detonate" refers to the VC's tactics of placing an electrically detonated primer in an explosive device, running an electrical cord some distance from it, and waiting for the prime time to detonate the device by using a low-voltage battery.

XVIII

The Reluctant POW

It was late January 1969 and by this time, I had commanded a rifle company in the Mekong Delta, some 60 miles south of Saigon, for more than three months. Earlier that day, my company had seen the last of a two-day stand-down. Although we had been on two-hour recall, the troops had enjoyed free time for showers, letter-reading and -writing, and a cookout with steak and beer. In midafternoon, all able-bodied troops loaded onto medium transport trucks for a trip to a designated drop-off point some 15 miles from the Ninth Infantry Division base camp. Our mission for the night was to establish a company-size ambush on a major canal junction and a couple of smaller tributaries to interdict enemy efforts to use the waterways for transporting men and materiel into our area of operations.

I was in the lead truck of the convoy, following the map of the area closely. After a 40-minute ride, I instructed the driver to stop at a crude, narrow trail that led to a small village nearby. I dismounted from the truck and told one of my radio operators to pass the word to dismount.

As usual, a collection of women and small children emerged from the village and began to hawk their wares. I was untrusting of such strangers because they usually brought marijuana and even heroin on occasion for sale to soldiers. I saw one woman with a batch of marijuana and yelled at her in Vietnamese to leave the area. One young boy had Vietnamese beer and Coca-Colas for sale. As soon as everyone had dismounted from the trucks, I ordered the company to assemble in platoon formation. Then I ordered the third platoon to take the point and lead us into the wooded jungle behind the village. Our objective area was about three kilometers from the village, and I planned to travel two kilometers during

XVIII. The Reluctant POW

daylight and move the remaining distance to the ambush sites after dark.

My third platoon was led by a staff sergeant. The platoon should have been led by a lieutenant or, in the absence of an officer, a more senior NCO. The last officer to lead the platoon had been severely wounded by a booby trap three weeks earlier, and there was a chronic shortage of senior NCOs to fill these leadership positions in my platoons.

Staff Sergeant Spanner, in his capacity as acting leader of the third platoon, had rounded up his men and struck out on a well-used trail whose crude logs over streams dictated movement by single file for the beginning of the route. Sergeant Spanner was a big-framed Indiana farm boy who, at this juncture, had been in the active army for only 18 months. Because of his exemplary performance on the battery of army aptitude tests, he had been selected to attend the Basic Noncommissioned Officer Course at Fort Benning, Georgia. The distinguished graduates of such courses were promoted immediately to the rank of staff sergeant. Under normal circumstances, it could take four or five years to achieve such rank. Yet here he was, out of necessity, in an officer's position as the acting platoon leader.

The remainder of the company fell in line and began moving through the small village toward the wooded area where I would assign flank security with the first and second platoons and have the mortar platoon bring up the rear. We had scarcely moved through the village when I heard an explosion about 100 meters ahead that sounded like a 40 mm grenade exploding. Soon after the explosion, Sergeant Spanner called on the radio.

"Charlie Six, this is Charlie Three, over." I took the handset from my radio operator on the company frequency and answered, "This is Charlie Six, over."

"Roger. My point man just shot at several Viet Cong as they ran from a hooch. He fired his M-79 at the group, wounding one of them. We also found a second man hiding in a hooch nearby. The man keeps pointing to his ears, apparently signaling that he doesn't hear. He also continues to say in broken English—'me no VC.' Since he doesn't have a South Vietnam government ID, we're holding both him and the wounded man."

"Roger, I'm moving toward your location now. Don't try to pursue the fleeing enemy. Just put out security in case there are other VC

Part 2—When Things Go Wrong in Combat

in the area. I'll bring Duc, our tiger scout,* to your location so that he can translate for us. Maybe we can get some intelligence information from these two captives."

My CP group and I moved hastily up the trail in Sergeant Spanner's direction. By the time we arrived, the third platoon medic had triaged the right foot of the injured VC guerrilla. After talking with the medic and confirming that the POW's wound was not life threatening, I turned to Sergeant Spanner. He was standing nearby examining the AK-47 rifle that the VC was carrying when he was spotted and engaged by the point man.

"Good work, Sergeant Spanner. Did this second man have a weapon?"

"No, sir. We've searched all three of the hooches in this cluster and haven't found any other weapons."

"OK. I'll have Duc ask them both some questions so that I can decide what to do with them. I can see that the wounded man will probably require a medevac."

I ordered the separation of the two captives, then I told Duc to talk to the wounded man and find out his unit, rank, and position within VC ranks. Duc proceeded to ask questions and listen intently to the man's answers. After several minutes, he turned to Sergeant Spanner and me and began to speak.

"He is like platoon sergeant in local VC squad. All men are from local area with family close to us here. He say that other man is not VC because he no can hear. VC not want man that no can hear. His squad is part of bigger unit, but he won't say name or number of bigger unit."

"Ask him how long he has been a VC."

Duc turned to the man again and spoke. After listening to the answer, he turned to me. "He say he VC for five years."

"Ask him if he knows the names of the other members of his squad."

Duc turned to the man yet another time and asked him several questions. After listening to the answers, he turned to me again.

---

*Tiger scouts were young Vietnamese men who had served with the VC and had found cause to abandon the insurgency. The South Vietnamese government put them through indoctrination training and English-language training and made them available to US forces as scouts. Their English skills were rudimentary but useful in dealing with the language barrier.

XVIII. The Reluctant POW

"Yes, Captain, he know all the names of his men, but he no say names."

Upon hearing the answers to Duc's questions, I decided that I must notify my battalion staff about the possible treasure trove of intelligence that could be extracted from the wounded VC. I turned to Sergeant Spanner and related my decision.

"OK, I've decided to do something that I dread. I must notify battalion headquarters that we have the POW and a detainee. By the way, I'm not convinced that the so-called deaf man is not a VC. I strongly suspect that he supports the local guerrillas in various ways. I'm concerned that when I notify battalion that we have these two men, they'll want to pick them up right away. That means that they'll send a helicopter to retrieve them, giving away our position to the enemy for miles around. So take some of your men and go up the trail to find an area that's open and large enough to land a chopper. If battalion wants to come and get these two, we'll be able to tell them that there's a suitable and secure area to land the chopper."

I notified my superior headquarters and within minutes was notified that the battalion intelligence sergeant would travel to our location in a light observation helicopter to retrieve the wounded POW. After receiving this order, I brought the second platoon forward and told its platoon leader to secure the open area that was about 100 meters from our current location.

The wounded POW was unable to bear weight on his wounded foot, so the tiger scout told the detainee to help him walk to the chopper's landing site. By the time the wounded POW could hobble the distance to the open area, we could hear the beating blades of the chopper. Sergeant Spanner and some of his men accompanied the two men to the landing site. My two RTOs and I also followed the group to the open area and watched the small chopper settle onto the ground a few meters from the trail.

The battalion intelligence sergeant emerged from the chopper as soon as it was settled on the ground. The pilot kept the engine at full throttle and the rotors at full revolutions per minute in anticipation of a quick departure. The intel sergeant walked over to me and said that he wanted only the POW to get into the rear seat of the chopper.

After hearing these words, I turned to Duc and told him to instruct the POW to get into the back seat. After Duc spoke a few words to the POW and the detainee, the two ambled laboriously to

Part 2—When Things Go Wrong in Combat

the chopper. With the aid of the detainee, the POW crawled into the chopper, at which time the intel sergeant motioned for him to slide to one side of the seat. The intel sergeant then proceeded to secure the safety harness around his body. So far, things had gone well.

While the intel sergeant was buckling the POW into the seat, the detainee jumped into the back seat and wrapped his arms around the intercom wires that hung from the ceiling—clearly signaling that he did not want to remain in the custody of frontline infantry troops.

I yelled to Duc to order him from the helicopter. Duc punched him in the arm to get his attention and yelled at him. The man screamed back in apparent defiance and held on to the wires. To add to the mayhem, several rounds of green tracers popped a few feet over the main rotor of the chopper. I shouted over the din for Sergeant Spanner to pull the defiant detainee from the chopper. He grabbed the small Vietnamese man and tried to pull him from the chopper without success.

A few more rounds cracked over the helicopter. I did not know why my superior headquarters wanted only the POW, but those were my marching orders. I turned again to Sergeant Spanner and said, "Get that son of a bitch out of that chopper. I don't give a damn how you do it. Just get him out, but don't shoot him."

That was all Sergeant Spanner needed to hear. He walked to the other side of the chopper and hit the rebellious man in his rib cage with the butt of his M-16 rifle. Without any further urging, the small man released the wires and jumped from the helicopter where he immediately fell to the ground, holding his side and gasping for breath.

The helicopter rose from the ground almost immediately and flew away safely. As soon as it had flown a safe distance, I instructed the mortar platoon to fire a volley of 60 mm mortar rounds across the clearing. Once the mortar rounds began exploding along the wood line, the firing ceased.

Frankly, I preferred to rid myself of prisoners or detainees as quickly as possible. Therefore, had the intel sergeant not deemed the detainee of little value, I would have left him in the chopper. Since he was required to stay behind, however, we had a detainee to guard until we could deliver him to the military police and the intelligence weenies.

I asked Sergeant Spanner to step aside so that we could have a private conversation. After we had moved a safe distance away, I

XVIII. The Reluctant POW

said, "I'm turning this detainee over to you. He is not to be viewed as a POW; however, he can be just as dangerous as a known POW. I expect you to treat him humanely. Don't mistreat him in any way, but bind him at night. When moving, bind his hands behind his back and keep him between two of your trusted men. If we must move at night, consider placing a rope around his neck. Any questions?"

"No, sir. As you know, I've guarded POWs in the past. I know not to trust them, so I'll keep an eye on this one."

Sergeant Spanner and I then returned to his platoon and my small CP group. We pursued my plan of movement to the ambush sites where I had the third platoon ambush the biggest canal, the first and second platoons ambush the two smaller canals, and the mortar platoon spread behind us for rear security.

We settled in for the night with the canals being observed by armed infantrymen with night vision sights. I sat leaning against a tree, speaking in a whisper with my senior medic about the condition of the detainee's rib cage, when my RTO on the battalion net called in a whisper to me, "Sir, it's the battalion commander on the radio for you." I crawled the few feet to my RTO and the radio and took the handset from him. "This is Charlie Six, over."

"Charlie Six, this is Mal Hombre Six. I have a couple of things for you. First, your element will participate in airmobile operations tomorrow. Be ready for pickup at 0600 hours. Mal Hombre Three will give you the location for pickup once I'm finished. As a heads-up, you should plan to continue airmobile operations for a second day. The second reason for my call is that I have been notified that two of our sister units have had POWs escape over the last three days. One unit apparently got complacent, and the POW grabbed a rifle from one of the soldiers and shot two soldiers before escaping. I'm aware that you have a detainee with you, and I'll relieve you of that responsibility when possible. In the meantime, make sure that your elements are vigilant and that they don't get complacent. I don't want to hear of you or your elements being killed or wounded by a POW or detainee. They'll take advantage of any opportunity to escape and they'll kill to accomplish it. Unless you have questions, I'll pass the radio handset to Mal Hombre Three."

"No, I don't have questions. Given your concerns about POWs, I'll ensure that our detainee doesn't escape and has no opportunity to harm us."

Part 2—When Things Go Wrong in Combat

Mal Hombre Three, who was the battalion operations officer, delivered a coded message that instructed us to return the following morning to the open area where the light observation helicopter had landed. After receiving the latter instructions, I decided to visit the third platoon and see how the detainee was being treated.

I spoke via the radio to Sergeant Spanner before approaching his location. As I arrived, I spotted the detainee sitting on the ground, covered with a poncho liner. I pulled the poncho liner back far enough to see that his hands were tied behind his back and that the rope binding his hands was also tied around a small tree.

I greeted Sergeant Spanner and sat on the ground near him. "Did you feed this guy when we stopped during the day?" "Yes, Sir. We gave him a couple cans of C-rations and some water. Then tonight, a couple of hours after sunset, he started complaining about being cold, so I covered him with my poncho liner. We plan to get him up every two to three hours and free his hands so that he can stimulate circulation and take a piss. He will be guarded by Corporal Smith, who will have an M-16 rifle at the ready and is itching for him to make even the slightest move to escape. Sergeant Braun, who was Smitty's best friend, was killed by a booby trap two weeks ago. Needless to say, Smitty is itching to settle the score. Oh, by the way, the little guy complained about mosquitoes biting him, so Smitty squirted some insect repellent on him and some of it spread to his private parts. He was moaning and groaning so much that we poured some water on his balls, but I know that it burned for several minutes. It was accidental. At least that's what Smitty told me."

I stared into Sergeant Spanner's eyes for a few seconds before responding. "OK. Everything you are doing so far is all right except for the insect repellent. We both know how that stuff burns. It will blister the poor bastard's balls and you know it, so don't let it happen again. By the way, we must stand to at 0500 hours and make our way to the same cleared area tomorrow morning for pickup for airmobile operations. The detainee will be a pain in the ass during these operations, so tie his hands behind his back and put a rope around his neck. Make sure that it doesn't choke him. I don't want him to escape. If we land on a hot LZ, you and your men won't have the luxury of being nice to a detainee. He'll just have to follow willingly or be pulled along."

The next morning, we made our way to the designated pickup

XVIII. The Reluctant POW

point at the appointed hour. We conducted airmobile operations for two exhausting days while ambushing assigned targets at night. Finally, on the third day, we were airlifted to Fire Support Base Moore, which was several miles from the Ninth Infantry Division base camp. This usually meant that we would have a couple of days to stand down, dry our feet, and get clean clothes. It also meant that we would have responsibility for securing the firebase perimeter. When the choppers landed at the fire support base, we were met by members of a military police unit who took custody of the detainee. I was relieved to transfer responsibility for him to the military police unit. I thought nothing of his appearance because we were all dirty, wet, and smelly. My men had removed the rope from his neck, yet a chafed ring was clearly visible and a large bruise remained on his left rib cage.

We remained at Fire Support Base Moore for two nights and three days. I had no further thoughts of the detainee until my battalion commander called me into his office in midafternoon on the third day. We exchanged small talk for a bit with him asking me how I felt. Then he delved into the real reason for calling me to his office.

"George, the POW that your guys captured has been a treasure trove of good intelligence. After considerable interrogation, the so-called detainee admitted to being a member of the same guerrilla unit. He was more active in the movement before an American artillery shell exploded near him and burst his eardrums. Your men deserve kudos for their actions. The treatment of the man who claimed to be a detainee is another matter. Once he was taken to the division rear area, he complained to the military police and intelligence officials that he was mistreated and beaten by your men. He claimed that his hands and feet were bound at night and that he was often tied to a tree. They've launched an investigation of you and anyone else who was involved in his care and treatment. Do you have anything to say about this issue?"

"Yes, Sir, I do! You told me, Sir, in no uncertain terms that I was not to let that man escape. Further, you cautioned me not to become complacent and let him or any other POW seize upon a weakness in our procedures and kill or maim any of my men in an escape attempt. We followed your guidelines and policies to the letter while conducting airmobile operations and executing ambushes at night. I don't expect noncombatants to understand or sympathize with the

Part 2—When Things Go Wrong in Combat

difficulties involved in guarding and protecting a POW or detainee under operating conditions. If you'll give me two hours to write a statement about this man's actions that jeopardized the lives of several Americans and threatened to damage or destroy a helicopter, I believe that you'll understand why and how he received the bruised ribs and the chafing around his neck. Also, sir, I request that you obtain a statement from the battalion intel sergeant. He witnessed the entire episode when the detainee jumped into the chopper and wrapped his arms around the intercom wires."

Lieutenant Colonel Patterson leaned forward in his chair while closing the folder in front of him. "Sure, George. Take the time that you need, but get the statement to me before you depart for the boonies later this afternoon."

Sergeant Spanner and I wrote statements beginning with our first contacts with the POW and detainee. Afterward, we exchanged statements and reviewed them for consistency, errors, or omissions. When I delivered them to Lieutenant Colonel Patterson, he informed me that the intel sergeant had written a comprehensive statement, focusing on the difficulties with the detainee around and in the chopper. He even permitted me to read the sergeant's statement. It was well written and corroborated the lion's share of the details that were contained in statements by Sergeant Spanner and me.

I was both pleased and relieved that I never heard anything else about the incident with the detainee. Additionally, when the first brigade commander visited my unit several weeks later, he mentioned that the intelligence information derived from the POW was very useful in eventually capturing or killing most of the remainder of the VC squad members.

XIX

Duck Boy

It was early spring 1969 in South Vietnam, where I was serving as commander of an infantry company of the Sixth Battalion, 31st Infantry Regiment, Ninth Infantry Division. My battalion commander informed me that my company would conduct a sweep of an area near the Mekong River and only a short distance from the division base camp during daylight, and ambush at least two canals overnight that flowed into the great river. Little did I realize that this operation would result in a troubling memory that would plague me indefinitely.

It seems that the enemy had succeeded recently in infiltrating rockets and 120 mm mortars into the area and using them to attack the division base camp. This area was familiar to us because we had conducted several sweeps of this type over the four months that I had commanded this company.

We were transported by truck from our area of the base camp to the dock on the Mekong River from which the U.S. Army conducted riverine operations. Some 50 of my men loaded onto two ACVs, and the remainder loaded into a landing craft, mechanized, mark 8, which appeared to be World War II vintage. We were soon underway with the convoy protected front and rear by patrol boats that were equipped with flame throwers. In addition, a potent aviation team supported us with a light observation helicopter, which we usually referred to as a LOCH, and an AH-1 Cobra attack helicopter. The additional support was welcome because my command group and I rode on one of the ACVs and were very exposed on its topside.

We reached our discharge point without incident and spread out with three rifle platoons abreast and the mortar platoon securing our rear. We were in radio contact with the pilots of the Cobra/LOCH team. By this time in the protracted war, the enemy had

Part 2—When Things Go Wrong in Combat

acquired good sniper rifles and trained some skillful marksmen and, on previous operations, had succeeded in killing one of my men and wounding two others. The presence of the Cobra and LOCH made it exceedingly difficult for snipers to shoot at us with impunity.

Booby traps were a constant threat, so we moved cautiously through the small clusters of peasant houses and rice paddies. This threat forced us to walk in the rice paddies and to avoid trails and rice paddy dikes. There was a serious downside to this policy, however, because it slowed our pace. In addition, walking in the deep, soft mud of the rice paddies was a serious drain on our energy.

The two helicopters would fly over our formation occasionally but usually flew ahead to ensure that any VC that might be in the area could not flee ahead of us and escape. The LOCH flew at treetop level while the Cobra flew at 300 or 400 feet.

By 0930 hours, we had traveled only one and a half kilometers because we were required to cross a major canal. Such crossings consumed valuable time because all canals for miles upstream in the Mekong River were affected by the South China Sea tides. Therefore, they had strong currents, and the canal banks were serious hazards because of the accumulation of deep mud. Such obstacles required us to place security on our flanks, send swimmers across with ropes, and then confiscate small boats (sampans) from peasants to use in crossing the strong currents. We were old hands at negotiating obstacles of this type, but putting safety first required methodical execution of our plan.

The crossing went smoothly, and once we were safely across and my platoon leaders had accounted for everyone, we continued on our sweep. Everything was business as usual until I heard the mini-gun of the LOCH shoot a blast of 7.62 mm bullets and monitored the subsequent verbal exchange between the two pilots.

"Whatcha got, Flanker 25?" the Cobra pilot queried excitedly.

"I just got a VC with my mini-gun. He had a pack and an AK-47. As you know, this is my first mission in the war zone, and that's my first kill. We need to celebrate this evening after these missions are done," the LOCH pilot responded.

"Roger that! You're off to a good start on your body-count log. By the time your tour of duty is over, your log should be full. By the way, what are those white things running around all over the place? They must be either chickens or ducks."

XIX. Duck Boy

"I don't know what they are. They were running all over the place ahead of that VC. Afraid of the chopper noise I suppose. Isn't that our purpose in supporting these grunts—to prevent the VC from escaping from their advance?"

About that time, I heard a loud explosion in the vicinity of my second platoon which was securing our right flank. The platoon leader contacted me immediately on his portable radio.

"Charlie Six, this is Charlie Two, over."

"Roger, this is Charlie Six, over."

"One of my men just hit a booby trap. He took considerable shrapnel in his lower extremities. My medic says that he should be evacuated ASAP because of heavy bleeding, over."

"Roger, I'll request a medevac right away. A quick look at the map indicates that there should be a cleared area about 100 meters to your north. Send five or six of your men to verify that a chopper can land there. If it's suitable, let me know. Then have your men secure it."

My senior medic, my two radio operators, and I wound our way slowly and carefully through the foliage to the second platoon CP. By the time we arrived, the wounded soldier was already on a makeshift litter and ready for transport to the pickup area. He was talking to some of his fellow soldiers about how the enemy had fooled him by placing a well-concealed second grenade near the visible one and how he felt foolish for tripping it.

I consoled him and wished him well before he was evacuated—knowing that such wounds guaranteed that he would not return to the war zone.

By the time we were ready to continue our sweep, we had been delayed nearly an hour. Since it was already 1100 hours and we had a lot of ground to cover by the end of the day, I ordered everyone to "move out."

About an hour later, I spotted a cluster of hooches that was familiar to us. On our previous operations in the area, we had become acquainted with one family that consisted of the mother and her son and daughter. She and her children appeared to be genuinely friendly, and the children practiced their limited English on us. On one operation, I traded some C-rations with the young boy for one of his ducks. Then I traded some C-rations with his mother in exchange for her agreement to clean and cook the duck with some rice. My

Part 2—When Things Go Wrong in Combat

radio operators and I also gave some chocolate bars to the two children, and I gave the mother some black pepper, salt, and sugar from my C-ration packets. The duck soup was very tasty, and the rice was probably the best I ever ate. The two children were charming and found a place in our hearts quickly. We saw the young boy several times on our sweeps through the area and began calling him Duck Boy.

As we approached the hooches, we could hear loud voices that were dominated by a female voice that sounded like someone wailing. I walked to the source of the commotion to find my first platoon leader trying to communicate with the mother with Duc, the Vietnamese tiger scout, translating. The mother's face was awash with tears. She looked pitifully distraught and was standing close to the lieutenant and banging her fists on his chest.

When I drew closer to the open area in front of her hooch, I discovered the source of her misery. The body of her son, whom we affectionately called Duck Boy, lay on a bamboo mat partially covered with a thin cloth. The cloth was soaked with blood, and the parts of his body that were visible revealed multiple bullet wounds. I felt shock, anger, and shame because I felt certain that the boy was the victim of the LOCH's mini-gun.

After the grieving mother opened her eyes enough to see me clearly, she recognized me and walked to me. She began pounding my chest with her clenched fists and speaking fast in Vietnamese. One of my radio operators moved quickly to pull the woman from me, but I waved him away. After a couple of minutes, she fell to the ground on her knees and began to nod and bow as if praying.

I turned to the tiger scout and asked him to translate what she had said to me and the lieutenant as she was pounding our chests.

In his broken English, he said, "She say VC kill the father of boy. Then she find new husband, who was father of girl, and VC kill him, too. Now the Americans kill her only son, and she no can have new son. She now old mamasan, and no man want old woman, so she must care for family without man. She also say today is boy's birthday. He 12 years today. She cook special duck eggs for him this day and tell him to stay away from military fighters who come past this place. She no understand why flying machine kill boy. He no have gun. He not man—he small boy. Americans should no kill boy. He was good boy, and he like Americans."

XIX. Duck Boy

I interrupted him at this point and asked him how she knew what happened to her son. He said that the boy herded the ducks close to one of the hooches in the area, and two old men witnessed the shooting. They said that the noise from the LOCH frightened the ducks, and when they scattered, Duck Boy ran after them.

I stood silent for several seconds, reminding myself to control my anger. I turned to my radio operator and motioned for him to give me the handset to his radio.

"Flanker 25, this is Charlie Six, over," I spoke into the mouthpiece.

"Roger, Charlie Six, this is Flanker 25, over."

"I'm located in the cluster of hooches to your south a distance of about 300 or 400 meters. The villagers have recovered the so-called Viet Cong fighter that you shot and killed near here. He is a 12-year-old boy who was wearing black pajamas, a white straw hat, and was carrying a bamboo stick for herding ducks. You made a horrible mistake, and I can't imagine what your excuse could be. You passed a stringent physical examination in order to qualify for flight school, so I assume that you have good vision. Of course, that doesn't account for your judgment. This incident will be emphasized in my after-action report tomorrow when I return to the rear area. These people are very poor, and that boy was everything to his mother. We know that he even helped look after the old people of this village. Those ducks were a vital resource for this family. They were one of the few things that they could take to market and trade for basic commodities."

"This is Flanker 25. He ran from us, so that gave me sufficient reason to consider him the enemy. As for my claim that he had an AK-47 rifle, it sure looked like one to me."

"This is Charlie Six. Running from you does not justify shooting him. We all have a responsibility to verify our target before pulling the trigger on a lethal weapon. Besides, he wasn't running from you—he was running to collect his frightened ducks. The people of this village have consistently exhibited pro–American sentiments. You have single-handedly set back relations between us Americans and these villagers to the point of making them hate us and possibly motivating them to cooperate with the enemy in killing us. Congratulations."

I turned to Duc and motioned with my hand for him to follow

me. I knelt beside the grieving mother and said, "On behalf of the United States Army, I apologize for this horrible mistake which has taken your son from you. My men and I were fond of your son and join you in grieving his loss. Please forgive us for this horrible mistake."

I stood and listened while Duc translated my words. The mother, who had risen from her knees, stood stone-faced, wiping tears. When Duc finished, she dropped to her knees again and began to pray.

After asking Duc what she said, he replied, "She say she pray to Buddha to protect her girl so she live to be woman someday. She say Buddha must protect boy, but he no do this. She say maybe she no pray to Buddha enough."

We continued our sweep and closed at twilight on the canals that we ambushed. During the early morning hours, my first platoon shot two VC in a sampan. We made no attempt to recover the enemy bodies or the contents of the sampan because the current was too strong.

We walked to our designated pickup point the following morning and rode to the Ninth Infantry Division base camp in army trucks. I filed a detailed report the next day about the incident involving Duck Boy. I never knew what action, if any, was taken against the overeager pilot. This unfortunate incident resulted in a haunting memory that still surfaces occasionally.

XX

The Rebellious Soldier

It was early February 1969 and I had commanded an infantry company in the Ninth Infantry Division for four months. This story begins in an unusual way, because the main character's background requires explanation. I learned early in my combat experiences to avoid getting too close to my subordinates—and even fellow officers—because if they became combat casualties, the closer the relationship, the deeper the pain. As the commander of this 133-man unit, I felt strongly that I should not be overly familiar with my subordinates. Although I much preferred to reward a soldier for good behavior and commendable actions, I still had the requirement to exact appropriate punishments when warranted. Yet there were those few times when a soldier endeared himself to me in such a way that I found my eagerness to know more of "what made him tick" to be compelling.

Let's call this young soldier Corporal Steve for the sake of conversation. I began to notice him soon after I assumed command of the company because he often volunteered to walk point for his platoon. Walking point was fraught with danger, yet he volunteered frequently to put himself in this vulnerable position. He was one of the best I had ever seen at walking point. He was quick to discover and engage the enemy, and he possessed amazing instincts regarding the presence of booby traps. I praised him on at least two occasions for his early detection of possible enemy ambush sites, which probably saved the company from mass casualties.

Steve was nearly 20 years old when I first met him, was about 73 inches tall, with a large frame and broad shoulders. Many of his troubles began early in life with placement in foster care at a young age. According to details that were shared with me by one of his sergeants, he was physically abused by his first foster care father. After running away twice and getting into trouble with law enforcement

Part 2—When Things Go Wrong in Combat

several times, he was dispatched by a judge to a juvenile detention center at the age of 14. Many of the other details of his early life came to me from his platoon sergeant. Steve explained to him that life in such a facility was no panacea. He said that because he was large for his age, every bully wanted to test him. These bullies would provoke him until he was forced to defend himself. Then, of course, such incidents usually ended with both boys either reprimanded or punished with restrictions on their activities or the denial of privileges.

Steve continued to have such troubles which were exacerbated by his obstreperousness—a character trait that tempted him to test authority and push boundaries. He "aged out" of the juvenile detention program upon reaching age 18. Given his stormy past, he was taken before a judge who advised him to volunteer for military service. Additionally, the judge warned him that should he come before his court again, he would risk a prison sentence. That's the "rest of the story" as to how I came to know details of his past.

My unit engaged in frequent air assault operations, and much of the time, we combat troops would assault onto a target and then sweep through the area for several kilometers searching for the enemy. Upon completion of the mission, we would be picked up either by helicopters for a follow-on assault or by trucks for transport to a fire support base or to the Ninth Infantry Division base camp where we frequently augmented the security force on the base perimeter.

The operation, which ultimately became a nightmare for Corporal Steve, began as a routine air assault mission onto a hot intelligence target. After arriving at the target, we found plenty of evidence that the enemy had occupied the area recently but had only used it as a short-term transit point. Enemy soldiers were very disciplined, deliberately and methodically masking evidence of their presence. For example, we found that they often dug shallow holes and buried the wrappers from their Chinese noodle packages. They never carelessly left behind usable military equipment, munitions, or explosives. The only grenades that they left behind were cleverly placed as booby traps. We found several booby traps during our sweep, and following my policy, we would explode them in place by pulling the pin on one of our grenades, laying it next to the booby-trapped one, and running away.

Much of what I have mentioned thus far was useful to the intelligence gatherers, so I summarized the known details of the enemy

XX. The Rebellious Soldier

strength as well as our best estimate of other important details into what would eventually become a verbal report to my higher headquarters. Given the number of holes we found with Chinese noodle wrappers, we estimated that at least 50 enemy fighters had occupied the target for at least one night. We also estimated that the enemy unit had occupied the target two nights before we arrived. I finished reporting this information to my battalion operations center only seconds before I heard my second platoon leader trying to contact me on our company radio. He sounded unusually excited.

"This is Charlie Six, over."

"This is Charlie Two. One of my elements just picked up a booby-trapped grenade. I can't for the life of me understand why he would do such a thing. I've ordered him to move away from everyone else in my platoon. He's just standing there, holding it and looking back at me. When he picked it up, the wire to which it was attached, pulled the firing pin. I've never seen him look so frightened and panicky as he does now."

I interrupted, saying, "This is Charlie Six. Tell him not to throw it. Tell him to hang on to it so we can figure out how to rid him of the grenade safely."

BAM! No sooner did my message end than I heard the explosion.

"Charlie Six, this is Charlie Two. My element threw the grenade just as you issued your order. We need a medevac urgently. That damned grenade had an instantaneous fuse. My element is gravely wounded. Over."

"Roger. I'll order one immediately. My senior medic is coming to your location to help with triage."

My radio operator, who monitored the frequency to my higher headquarters, requested a medevac. He had no sooner placed the order than I received a radio transmission from a helicopter. Fate had surely sided with Corporal Steve because the chopper was a medevac that was returning to the evacuation hospital at the Ninth Infantry Division base camp.

"Charlie Six, this is Triage 29 Alpha. I monitored your request for medevac and heard your coordinates. I'm within five minutes of your location. Pop smoke and secure a landing zone."

"This is Charlie Six. Roger. My platoon is in the process of securing an LZ. I'll instruct them to pop smoke immediately. However, request that you wait for my clearance to land. Over."

Part 2—When Things Go Wrong in Combat

"Roger. This is Triage 29 Alpha. I identify yellow smoke. I'll be there in three minutes and will fly around slowly until I get the OK from you to land."

Within five minutes, the second platoon leader gave me an all clear for the medevac to land. I made no attempt to make my way to the LZ and wish this wounded soldier God speed. My presence was not necessary, and we had already discovered several other booby traps in this area. While waiting for my senior medic to return and share the details of the wounded soldier's injuries, my thoughts were dominated with the why questions that usually accompany such incidents. After seeing the helicopter fly away, I contacted the second platoon leader and asked him to give me the wounded soldier's roster number, which was a system we used to identify men assigned to my company without revealing names over the air. I was both shocked and puzzled to learn that it was Corporal Steve. Soon after this discussion, my senior medic rejoined my CP group and described the nature and extent of Steve's wounds.

"Sir, he released the grenade in an overhand throwing motion, and the grenade exploded instantly. The platoon leader told me that the enemy apparently removed the powder from the four-second fuse channel. The shrapnel hit him in his face and neck and penetrated his chest. He had very serious hemorrhaging in his lungs, and he may have injuries to other internal organs. Sir, only God's intervention can save this man's life. He was already struggling for breath when they loaded him into the chopper."

I was deeply troubled and saddened to hear the details of an incident that should never have happened. Corporal Steve had consistently done so many things right—applying sound logic and good judgment to his actions. Why this?

My unit returned the following day to the Ninth Infantry Division base camp for a two-day stand-down. After settling in and attending to several administrative and logistical issues, I decided to go to the evacuation hospital to visit Corporal Steve. The company first sergeant had made several phone calls to the hospital and inquired about the soldier's welfare. He was told repeatedly that Corporal Steve was in critical condition and that visitors were not allowed. He was also told that our wounded soldier would be evacuated out of Vietnam as soon as he was stabilized.

My driver delivered me to the hospital in the late morning. I

XX. The Rebellious Soldier

went directly to the ICU, and after explaining that I was Corporal Steve's commander, the nurse told me that I could enter. A doctor approached and told me to follow him. I was grateful for the assistance because there were multiple men in the ICU with bandages, tubes, and other devices attached making identification difficult.

After a short distance, we approached a bed that had Corporal Steve's name on it. Upon seeing him, I felt a sharp pain in my gut. Obviously, that was my first opportunity to see the many shrapnel wounds on his face, upper torso, and right hand and arm.

The doctor stopped me several feet from Steve's bed and turned to face me before speaking. "Captain, he's under the influence of a lot of pain drugs. He can't interact with you in any way and will have no memory of your visit. Please keep your distance because his potential for infection is very high. He's a fighter or he never would have survived thus far. I met the medevac that delivered him to the hospital, and I could see that his body was actually shutting down when he arrived. I had in my possession a special instrument that we use in dire circumstances for draining blood from lungs. He has undergone multiple surgeries thus far and is slated for yet another one this afternoon. As you can surmise, we have struggled to stabilize him sufficiently to place him on a flight to the next level of care. You're welcome to observe him as much as you like, but he will likely have no memory of it. He'll be under sedation for the duration of his stay with us. His pain level is very high."

I said a little prayer under my breath and left the hospital. I returned to see Corporal Steve the following morning at which time the head nurse told me that he was improving and that there was every reason to believe that he would survive. She also said that he would be on a flight that afternoon for Japan.

I know that this unfortunate soldier survived because fellow veterans who live in California near him have shared with me details of conversations with him. I have not attempted to contact him because hearing from me might be the kind of trigger that releases the ghosts that he and other vets keep locked away. I am confident that his road to recovery was long and painful and that he has wished a thousand times that he had not thrown that grenade.

XXI

When Superiors Make Mistakes

It was early March 1969 and I was the commander of a rifle company in the Ninth Infantry Division about 60 miles south of Saigon. My unit had returned the previous day to the Ninth Infantry Division base camp for a two-day stand-down. When we had such opportunities, our supply sergeant treated us occasionally to a barbecue cookout with steaks or hamburgers and beer. As usual, I had very little idle time because of the numerous diversions awaiting me in the rear area. We were nearly always on a two-hour recall status during these stand-downs, so I rarely left the unit area.

It was the afternoon of our first full day of stand-down. The supply sergeant and a couple of recovering wounded soldiers cooked hamburgers, so we feasted on this delightful cuisine while drinking a cold beer. Sundown was fast approaching when I received a call to report immediately to the battalion TOC. I grabbed my cap, and while walking hurriedly to the battalion headquarters, I reminded myself that such a call usually meant that my company was about to be alerted for deployment in its capacity as the battalion's immediate-reaction force.

As soon as I entered the battalion TOC, the operations officer spread a map on a small table and began pointing to an area and describing an alarming situation that was still unfolding. He said that a company from a sister battalion of the first brigade had walked into an ambush by a major VC force. He explained that the confirmed details indicated that the company commander was dead and that there were several more soldiers killed or wounded. In addition, several weapons and other equipment had been lost and could not be recovered at that time because of enemy fire and a grass fire that was ignited by rocket-propelled grenades.

XXI. When Superiors Make Mistakes

As he continued with the briefing, he handed me an operations order with the frequency and radio call sign of the distressed unit. He explained that my unit would be inserted near the besieged unit and that we were to retrieve all the wounded and dead and recover as much of the weapons and equipment as possible. He also emphasized that the brigade commander was inserting other units around the VC unit in an effort to trap it within a cordon and that we were to prevent the enemy soldiers from escaping.

I hurried back to my company area and told the first sergeant to notify all of the platoon leaders and platoon sergeants to come to the unit orderly room immediately. While waiting for the first sergeant to round up these leaders, I notified my radio operators to get new radio batteries, water, and rations for at least three days. I also notified my supply sergeant to issue C-rations for three days. When my subordinate leaders arrived, I briefed them on the mission and told them that we were not allowed two hours; instead, we must be on the division helipad ready to go within one hour. I released everyone promptly with my order to be ready to load onto trucks within 45 minutes for the short trip to the division helipad.

My subordinates rounded up as many of their men as possible within the abbreviated period. When we consolidated to load onto the transport trucks, I ordered my platoon leaders to make a list of those present for the operation. We took a head count and determined that we had 90 men of a possible 122.

The choppers arrived within minutes of our arrival at the helipad. My two radio operators and I, my artillery forward observer and his radio operator, and my senior medic loaded onto the first helicopter. As we flew to our destination, I studied the terrain as much as possible. My ability to follow the terrain closely was hampered by the fading light. In fact, darkness had enveloped us by the time we reached our LZ. As soon as the remainder of my company disembarked from the choppers, I instructed my platoons to place security in a perimeter around the company.

I did a quick survey of our physical environment. We were inserted in an open area that showed no signs of being inhabited. There was a tree line about 250 meters to our north; otherwise, the LZ was relatively flat with grass nearly waist high.

After making a few mental notes, I instructed my radio operator on the company radio net to dial the frequency of the troubled unit

Part 2—When Things Go Wrong in Combat

to try and make contact with them. I stood nearby as he dialed the unit's frequency on his portable radio and began calling, using their call sign. When there was no response, I instructed him to install the longer antenna on his radio. He complied and began repeating their call sign on the prescribed frequency. From my perspective, we should have been able to communicate well—assuming that their radio was undamaged and in operating condition because I was told that we would be inserted directly behind the unit.

After we had been on the ground 10–15 minutes, we began to hear M-16 rifle fire. Because the rounds were high, they did not pose an immediate threat. To prevent a possible friendly-fire exchange, I instructed my platoons to "hold their fire." We had been advised that other friendly units were also to deploy to the area, so there was a chance that the shots were coming from them.

I notified my battalion commander that I had not succeeded in communicating with the troubled unit. I also reported that M-16 rounds were being fired over our heads but that my unit was under my order to not return fire. I also explained that we were situated in high dry grass that would burn fast if ignited.

The next communication came not from the battalion commander but from his operations officer.

"Charlie Six, you've been inserted in the wrong place. You're approximately four kilometers from the target area. We've already requested to use the division choppers again immediately to pick up your company and reinsert you in the proper place. So round up your men and arrange them in chopper-load order. The choppers are inbound to your location now. When they arrive, one of them will discharge a smoke screen, after which the lift ships will land immediately to pick up your company. Any questions?"

"This is Charlie Six. Roger. First, can you do anything to stop the M-16 fire from our north? The rounds are barely over our heads now, and I don't want to deal with such a threat when the choppers arrive. Also, I need some time to recover my men and account for everyone. I placed security out 360 degrees at a distance of 50 meters."

"Roger. This is Chestnut Three. Move with haste. This is a priority mission and your unit is needed urgently."

After ordering my platoon leaders to round up their men, I further instructed them to account for everyone and inform me when every man was recovered and ready for the next phase.

XXI. When Superiors Make Mistakes

Before I received a heads-up from my platoon leaders, I heard the chopper blades beating the air as they flew in our direction. This made me nervous because I was well aware of the expectations from my superiors. They had made a big mistake and were trying desperately to recover from it with grace.

I had received a heads-up from all but my third platoon. The platoon leader reported that he could account for all but one man. I challenged him by asking if he was certain that the man had accompanied us on the mission. He responded emphatically that the man had indeed accompanied us.

In the meantime, the helicopters were circling to our south awaiting the order to land and pick up my company. This situation presented me with a huge dilemma. There was never any question about leaving one of my men. My challenge was how to delay this flight of helicopters without inviting the wrath of my commander.

Twice I had to request that the choppers be held up by stating truthfully that I could not account for one man. I was unable to escape the thought that one of the M-16 rounds might have struck him and he lay dead in the tall grass. Finally, after nearly putting me in cardiac arrest, my third platoon leader reported that they had found the man sleeping in the high grass. I was relieved to say the least, but my vindictive nature prompted me to say, "Make damn certain that you make him understand that he never again puts the rest of his fellow soldiers in such a situation."

The unwelcome M-16 fire abated minutes before a single chopper flew low over us and discharged a thick smoke screen. The lift ships followed immediately, and soon afterward, my first and second platoons and my CP group were traveling to the target area.

As the choppers slowed and began descending, I was relieved to see illumination rounds hanging in parachutes over the area. With this light, I could see that the area contained a lot of dry rice paddies and a few scattered peasant hooches. I caught the scent of burning grass or woods, but no blazing fire was visible.

As soon as we landed, I ordered the two platoon leaders to place men 360 degrees around us and wait for my orders to move. I then instructed my radio operator to repeat the effort to make contact with the survivors of the ambushed unit. I was relieved that the response was immediate. I took the handset from my RTO and began to coordinate a link-up with the other unit. Once I realized that they were little more than 100 meters from us, I asked them to send a few men to us as we waited for the remainder of my company to arrive by lift ships.

As we waited for the men from the other unit to reach us, a medevac chopper landed about 300 meters from us—obviously picking up the wounded and dead. Within a few minutes, men from my first platoon escorted a staff sergeant and two other men into my position. What the sergeant reported was disconcerting.

He said that the delay in our arrival had forced the survivors of his unit to evacuate the dead and wounded without additional help. He emphasized, however, that they were forced to leave several weapons and other items of equipment at the ambush site because the enemy had that area covered with automatic weapons fire. He also stated that they were in frequent engagements with enemy soldiers who were trying to escape the encircled area. I asked him if he and his men had urgent needs. He responded that they were short of water because medics had used much of it to wash wounds. We collected several full canteens and gave them to the two men with the sergeant.

At that time, the third platoon and the mortar platoon arrived and rejoined the company. We immediately followed the men from the ambushed unit to their position. As my men shared food and stories with some of the men, I asked a lieutenant from the ambushed unit to brief me on the situation. He revealed that he and the other survivors were waiting for pickup by helicopter to be flown to the rear area. He stated that according to his orders, our arrival relieved them of responsibility to plug the gap in the encirclement. He emphasized that because he and the other survivors were forced by a grass fire to retreat to their present location, the enemy was exploiting this situation to escape the cordon.

After the briefing by the lieutenant, I called my platoon leaders to my location and described my strategy. My first order was to the artillery forward observer attached to my company. I told him to order illumination rounds both behind and in front of the gap. Such a strategy would eliminate the shadow effect that accompanies such suspended light sources. Since we had to cover approximately one kilometer to link up with units on our right and left, I placed the first and second platoons abreast as we began to move into the area and make contact with adjacent units. We did not move far before all

XXI. When Superiors Make Mistakes

hell broke loose. It soon became clear that individual enemy soldiers were trying to sneak past us. As soon as they were discovered, some of them would raise their weapons over their heads and surrender. We took them prisoner and quickly moved them to the third platoon which was providing rear security. Those who did not surrender were neutralized. Conditions forced us to move slowly and cautiously because the men were reporting the presence of booby traps. As we drew near the original ambush site, the enemy fire became intense—signaling the presence of a larger consolidated force. I held up my forward elements and ordered the artillery forward observer to call for artillery support with 105 mm high-explosive rounds.

My intent was to force our way into the area where the equipment had been abandoned. However, before we could accomplish the task, I was ordered to pull back 100 meters because a bombing mission that would involve napalm and high-explosive bombs was on order.

We complied by pulling back from the engagement with the enemy force and waiting for the air attack. As soon as the first fighter dropped high-explosive and napalm rounds into the encirclement, the enemy force panicked and some of its elements decided to fight their way out through my company.

My company and the adjacent friendly units to our right and left fought and killed enemy troops most of the night. With the help of the 105 mm artillery support, we succeeded in holding our part of the line and preventing the enemy from escaping. In defending our sector, several of my soldiers were wounded, but no one was killed. We entered the area of the initial ambush the following morning and found that the enemy had indeed captured two M-60 machine guns and several M-16 rifles when they ambushed the American unit. However, we and the on-call support units killed the enemy troops before they could evacuate their booty.

By the way, the following morning I saw the soldier who was found asleep, and he was sporting a bruised eye. Ultimately, he became one of my best soldiers and, over several weeks, earned my respect. Nothing more was said about the sleeping incident and its potentially grave consequences.

XXII

Stealth Mission

It was late March 1969 and I was still commanding a rifle company of the Sixth Battalion, 31st Infantry, Ninth Infantry Division in the Mekong Delta. I have written a lot about the types of missions my company was assigned. The other line companies of the battalion were rotated among these various missions, and it was easy, it seemed, to settle into a routine that enabled the enemy to pattern our behavior. I sensed it, and so did one of my senior NCOs. When the battalion was assigned the security mission for the Ninth Infantry Division base camp, my company was frequently assigned to the same general area and was ordered to enter it during daylight hours, stay the night, and then exit the following morning. We were transported by trucks each time to the same peasant village, and from there, we walked about two kilometers into the area where we ambushed major trails and a large canal. On previous trips into the area, we were shot at by snipers, ambushed by automatic weapons, and traumatized twice by 60 mm mortars. After shooting or lobbing mortars at us, the enemy had plenty of time to escape and prevent us from exacting our revenge. We always returned fire and even fired our own 60 mm mortars at them, but we rarely knew if we were effective in killing or wounding them.

My company had been the security force at Fire Support Base Moore for two days and two nights where, among other things, we were able to shower, receive clean, dry clothes, and dry our feet. In midmorning on our last day, I was called to the TOC, where I knew I would receive our next mission assignment. After entering the sandbagged bunker, my battalion commander wasted no time in explaining the mission and its purpose. Our targeted area was the same locale to which we had been assigned numerous times, and it was for the same reasons. The VC continued to shoot mortars and rockets

XXII. Stealth Mission

from the area into the Ninth Infantry Division base camp, and the division commander insisted that we find a solution to it.

When I returned to my CP group, I instructed my radio operator to ask all platoon leaders and platoon sergeants to come to our bunker. After they arrived, I briefed them on the mission. As they were leaving the bunker, one of my senior NCOs lingered in the doorway and asked if I had a minute to hear a proposal. This NCO was a consummate professional whom I liked and respected and valued his advice, so I was quick to agree.

"Sir, I've been thinking about this next mission. I know I don't have to convince you of the hazards of operating as usual in that area. The enemy can detect our presence a full half kilometer away, which allows them to plant booby traps, shoot at us, or drop mortars on us. Can you persuade the battalion commander to permit us to enter that area at night and stay at least three days? We know that local Viet Cong guerrillas visit their mamasans at night, so I believe we can catch them in the hooches and kill or capture some of them. Then we can pull one of your favorite stunts after the first day by making it appear that we're pulling back from the canal, yet leave a squad-size force to ambush it again at night."

I told him that I loved the idea and thanked him for bringing such tactics to my attention. I also promised that I would approach the battalion commander and seek his approval. Although we had used stealth to surprise the enemy on a previous mission into this area, we had not tried to catch the VC in their hooches at night.

I went to the battalion TOC and requested to speak with the battalion commander. After he invited me into his office, I appealed to him for a modification to the mission. "Sir, you know that that's a difficult and dangerous area. I'm not complaining, but I'm making the case to modify the way we operate. Might I suggest that we be dropped off by trucks within easy striking distance of the area and be allowed to wait until after dark to make our way into the remote villages and canals? Maybe the guerrillas won't see us coming and have time to alert their comrades and seed our paths with booby traps or fire mortars at us as they've done in the past. Also, Sir, I'm convinced that we could be far more effective if we could remain in the area for several days."

I was surprised when he questioned my motivation to change the timing and duration of the mission. I made my best pitch succinctly and impressively—at least, I thought so.

Part 2—When Things Go Wrong in Combat

"I've been training my men to go quietly when we move and to hide out during the daytime. Our plan is to be better than the VC at his game. We want to kill him in his own bed at night and surprise him totally during the day by behaving unlike typical American troops. The risk is greater than the reward, sir, if you order us into the area during daylight hours and pull us out the following day."

After consultation with the battalion operations officer, the battalion commander agreed to my proposal. It was both gratifying and reassuring to have the chance to change our timing and methods and maybe thin the enemy ranks. Within a few hours, we were transported by trucks along one of the few roads in that region to an outpost to wait for darkness. Since we had about two and a half hours of waiting time, we ate some C-rations and rested. Afterward, I called the four platoon leaders to my location and briefed them on the plan.

I told them that we would move with platoons in file. The first platoon would be on point in the center, the second platoon would secure the left flank, the third platoon would secure the right flank, and the mortar platoon would secure the rear. My command group would follow the first platoon. I advised them that the distance to our ambush site was slightly more than five kilometers and that it would take most of the night to reach it. After the line platoons were instructed to set up platoon-size ambushes once we reached the site, the mortar platoon was given the task to provide rear security and be ready to reinforce the action as directed by me. I told them that we would rest in the daytime and man the ambushes at night. Since we had been in the area multiple times, most of the men were familiar with the locations of the hooches along the route. Likewise, they knew that they should use all the stealth they could muster in approaching them. I also shared my assumption that the VC guerrillas would visit their mamasans at night after hiding out all day, and we should be able to catch them in the hooches.

As dusk fell, we began moving from the peaceful outpost toward the targeted area. For the first two kilometers, we traveled on an old roadbed that had been constructed by the French during their occupation. Although it was severely eroded in some places and reduced to hardly more than a trail in others, it allowed the point platoon to move quietly and quickly. The peasants had actually built hooches astride the old roadbed in places, so the leading elements from the

XXII. Stealth Mission

first platoon could be inside the hooches with their rifles at the ready before the peasants could react or flee.

We were disappointed that the search of the first two hooches produced the usual old mamasans and a couple of middle-aged

A typical peasant hooch in the Central Highlands. Notice that the walls and roof are stronger and thicker than hooches in the south because the temperature could drop to chilling levels, especially in the mountains at night.

Part 2—When Things Go Wrong in Combat

Typical peasant hooch in the Mekong Delta. During the rainy season, most of the land in our area of operation was covered with water as shown in this photograph. The wet conditions made it impossible to keep our feet dry, which frequently resulted in immersion foot.

Another typical peasant hooch in the Mekong Delta.

XXII. Stealth Mission

women with several small children. I was beginning to doubt my cunning when I heard the unmistakable sound of automatic weapons fire which came from the trail ahead of my command group. I saw a dim light shining from a peasant hooch nearly 100 meters ahead. As if he could read my thoughts, my radio operator handed me the radio handset.

Indeed, I was anxious to know what had transpired, so I called the first platoon leader. "Whatchagot, Charlie One Six?"

"We found two VC suspects in this hooch, Charlie Six. One ran and we fired on him. We've detained the second one. He doesn't have an ID and appears to be sick because he's got a cloth tied over his mouth, over."

"Did you kill the one that ran, over?"

"Negative, but we know we hit him because we found a blood trail leading from the hooch. We also found two AK-47 rifles and two military packs with ammo next to the bed."

Given the lack of details about the detainee, it appeared prudent to delay calling in a SITREP to battalion operations. After instructing Lieutenant Johnson to secure the immediate area and wait for me to catch up, I also instructed the second and third platoons to rest in place as best they could. They had the toughest routes because they were sloshing through knee-deep mud in rice paddies while some of us walked on firm ground some of the time.

I complimented the lieutenant as I approached and asked if his medic had taken a look at the detainee.

"This man appears to be pretty sick, sir. My medic took his temperature a few minutes ago, and it was 103."

"What does your tiger scout say about this man? Except for his sickness, he appears to be able-bodied, and of course, we've traveled this route many times and we've never seen him or any other man at this hooch," I asked, anticipating that my superior headquarters would want to know such details.

"Duc says that he is a local Vietcong guerrilla and is probably related to the other people who were in the hooch with him."

I hesitated a few minutes before calling in a SITREP to battalion in order to collect my thoughts. I really wanted to rid myself of this sick detainee. Burdening one of my platoons with guarding a detainee, especially a sick one, would not be a well-received task. My assumption was that this man was potentially as dangerous as any

Part 2—When Things Go Wrong in Combat

other prisoner. Besides, we neither knew the source of his illness nor if it was contagious.

I called in a SITREP, reporting the detainee and other details regarding our actions at the hooch. My report included the fact that the tiger scout considered the detainee to be a member of the local guerrilla unit. I was anxious for battalion operations to know our location because of the shots fired by the first platoon. I emphasized that the detainee was sick and that I preferred to leave him at the hooch—despite the fact that our tiger scout concluded that he was a VC guerrilla. Besides, our intent from the outset was to check all peasant hooches along our route early in the night and then move stealthily to our ambush site, planning to maintain ambushes on the canal for two more nights and parts of three days. My plea fell on deaf ears. The intelligence staff officer insisted that we hang on to the man until we could either medevac him or turn him over to the military police upon our return to the ninth division base camp.

The company moved out along the planned route, but I held my command group in place long enough for the mortar platoon to reach us. I turned over the detainee to them. The mortar platoon leader was very unhappy about my decision.

We continued making our way deeper into the area. We took a short break at 0230 hours because everyone was suffering from exhaustion, especially the second and third platoons. Our tactics had proven successful. The first platoon's point man and his backup had killed three VC. They had even shot two of the enemy in their beds. That was exciting news to those of us seeking revenge for the many booby traps and ambushes by the local guerrillas. I, too, welcomed a break and was leaning against a tree when I overheard my radio operator speaking to the sergeant who was the acting mortar platoon leader. After the brief verbal exchange, my radio operator approached me and offered me the handset, saying, "Charlie Four Six says the prisoner died, Sir."

I took the handset and responded right away. "Charlie Four Six, this is Charlie Six. What's happening with the prisoner? Over."

"My men said that he just died as we were crossing the last swampy area, over."

Before answering, I remembered that the water was surprisingly deep and that short troops were required to get on the backs of taller ones.

XXII. Stealth Mission

My response was, "Yeah, I'll bet he just died. I see a light ahead; there must be a hooch there, so tell your men to bring his body to that location. We can at least drop it off with the locals instead of simply leaving it out in the swamp. I don't want them to think that we killed him."

As I pondered what I would report to battalion operations, I reminded myself of the importance to the intelligence operatives of interrogating this probable VC guerrilla. We had already made the detainee's capture a matter of record, so we would be expected to safeguard and deliver him to our higher headquarters for final disposition. So it was with trepidation that I instructed my radio operator to report the prisoner's demise. After he complied, I took that to be the end of discussion about the dead man.

I gave myself a mental thrashing for placing the detainee in the custody of the mortar platoon, reminding myself of the fate of several prisoners who "ran" while in the custody of my subordinates. I was well aware of the pent-up frustrations among the men at not being able to exact punishment in kind on the enemy in those instances where booby traps maimed or killed our fellow soldiers. This frustration often translated into the urge to kill enemy prisoners, especially in those instances where we were required to guard them and drag them along for long periods. I remembered also that I had suppressed the urge to lash out at prisoners on several occasions or even to kill them, so I understood this phenomenon.

We continued on a direct course to the assigned area where we would ambush canals. I knew from map analysis that we would traverse a swampy area. The going was slow because we had to travel without the benefit of illumination. After all, we were in the midst of guerrilla territory and it could be very dangerous to use lights.

My first platoon leader notified me that his men had traveled beyond the hooch with the glowing light. As my CP group approached the hooch, I halted everyone except the mortar platoon so that we could wait long enough for me to examine the corpse.

As I approached the hooch, I observed that there was a single, old mamasan sitting on a crude stool with a large candle on a table nearby. Before her on the ground was a very large, solid white sow with what appeared to be more than 10 piglets. When I stopped long enough to count them, the actual count was 13. The woman was rotating them among the sow's teats to ensure that each one received a nourishing amount of milk.

Within about 15 minutes, two members of the mortar platoon arrived with the corpse. I asked if they were assigned the task of guarding the man. After they confirmed that they were assigned that particular task, I bent down and rolled the man onto his back. I examined him carefully for any evidence of physical abuse, such as bruises or cuts on his face, head, or neck. After finding no evidence of abuse, I placed both hands on his chest and pushed gently. Water gushed out of his mouth.

"Just died, huh?" I nearly shouted. "Either you drowned him or you let him drown, dammit, and you know it," I stated as I looked into my subordinate's eyes. "Take him into this hooch and leave him. This old woman will know what to do. I'll deal with you two later."

As I walked away, my radio operator on the battalion frequency approached and said that the battalion duty officer wanted to speak to me.

I responded immediately. "This is Charlie Six, over."

"Roger, Charlie Six. This is Rhinestone 33. Higher-up has been informed about the prisoner's demise, and he says you should put a bullet hole in the corpse so we can count it in our weekly body count."

I was very upset and angry at such an outlandish suggestion. By this time, it was about 0400, and I was extremely tired. Maybe that is why I responded as I did.

I said, "I'll do no such damn thing. How in the hell does this square with these locals who saw us take this man from his hooch alive? We say on the one hand that we're trying to win their hearts and minds, yet you suggest that I should put a bullet hole in the corpse so we can include it in our body count. I'd be embarrassed to do it myself, and I sure as hell won't order my men to do it."

I knew that several of my men heard enough of the duty officer's words to understand the substance of our conversation. I turned to the men nearest me and said, "Men, I'm sorry that you heard what I said. You've been witness to two bad examples. First, the duty officer ordered me to put a bullet hole in a corpse. Second, you heard me refuse to obey an order, which supposedly came from a superior officer. I'm deeply troubled and embarrassed over this incident. Put yourselves for a moment in the position of these poor, helpless

XXII. Stealth Mission

peasants. I can't conceive of any justification for going back in that hooch and shooting a corpse, and I want this issue to die right here and now."

It took us the rest of the night to travel the last one and a half kilometers. There were no trails, so the first platoon had to break trail the entire distance. Also, there were two swamps that contained bodies of water that were quite deep. In fact, the water level in one of the swamps was up to my chin.

It was well after daylight by the time we closed on our targeted canals. I was exhausted and knew that my men could use some well-earned rest. I called my platoon leaders to my location and issued guidance for the time that we would spend at that site. I instructed them to keep their men at least 50 meters from the two canals and to be quiet for the rest of the day. I also told them to wait until dark before moving to the canal banks and to withdraw from them before daylight the following morning. I explained that from previous missions of this type, the enemy would search thoroughly and cautiously to locate us and that we must not make it easy for him. After the meeting, I found myself a suitable piece of ground and laid down for some rest with my legs extended and my head resting on my pack.

After about four hours, I awoke and heated some C-ration beans and franks. In midafternoon, I called the platoon leaders to my location once again and issued guidance for the night ambush. My plan was to position the first and second platoons on the big canal and the third platoon on the smaller one. The mortar platoon had its usual mission of rear security. Everyone was allowed to rest for the remainder of the day.

I deliberately stayed awake and alert during the early hours of the night because an incoming tide was flowing strongly and those were ideal conditions for movement by sampan—assuming that it was flowing in the desired direction. Since the tide shifted direction about every five hours, I knew that there would be a strong outgoing tide after midnight. I called my platoon leaders and shared my belief that the best time for the enemy to travel the canals would be on the outgoing tide.

The first half of the night was calm and disappointing, so I laid on the ground for some rest. I think I must have been dozing at about 0100 hours when troops of the third platoon opened fire with M-60

Part 2—When Things Go Wrong in Combat

machine guns and M-79 grenade launchers. A few green tracers zipped through the trees well above our heads, which signaled that the enemy fighters in the sampan were able to get a few shots off. After less than a full minute, the firing stopped. I could hear voice commands coming from the platoon's area, so I roused my radio operators, senior medic, and artillery forward observer and directed them to follow me.

When we reached the ambush site, the men were pulling two wounded VC fighters from the sampan. Two more lay dead on the bank nearby. It was a large sampan with a crude, small cuddy on its bow. It was riddled with bullet holes and had at least one large hole in its bow where an M-79 grenade must have hit it. As I drew nearer, I could hear female voices from inside the cuddy. One of the troops had boarded the sampan and was clearing what he described as a sinking boat. After helping the second woman from the wreckage, he declared it clear and ready to sink. Given the amount of damage to the sampan from the third platoon's weapons, I expected to see blood dripping from both women, but they appeared to have escaped the brutal attack.

In my view, they were all prisoners. The women had no government identification and they were in the company of verifiable enemy fighters, so we classified them all as prisoners. I turned the women over to the mortar platoon and instructed the platoon leader to move them away from the canal. As soon as it appeared that everything associated with the ambush was completed, I ordered everyone to move away from the canal bank. We had given away our location with all of the firing and commotion, and there was reason to be concerned about a possible sniper attack. Furthermore, I did not savor the thought of calling a medevac for the wounded VC, so I asked my senior medic for his assessment of their wounds. I was very relieved when he told me that their wounds were not life threatening and that they could wait until the following day for evacuation.

After things grew calmer and quieter, I laid down once more for some rest and fell asleep right away. About two hours later, I heard several rounds of M-16 fire from the first platoon area; then M-60 machine gun fire erupted. After a few seconds, the firing stopped, and I began to hear voices.

I jumped up, grabbed my M-16 rifle, and told my radio operators to follow me. When we reached the canal, there was no sampan and

XXII. Stealth Mission

no visible enemy. The platoon leader soon appeared and explained that Mouse was on watch with an M-16 rifle, which had a starlite scope mounted on it.* He spotted the sampan as it sped down the canal with the fast-flowing tide and killed both VC very quickly with only a few shots. The sampan was still floating and entangled in some brush near the opposite bank, so the platoon leader ordered the machine gunner to shoot it full of holes so it would sink.

The next morning, everyone except the mortar platoon was in a jubilant mood. It seems that the women prisoners squirmed and complained much of the night about having their hands and feet bound with a rope. When I asked the platoon leader if he allowed the women to have bathroom breaks, he explained that they were untied and led away from everyone by an armed guard. I asked if they ever attempted to flee, and he said, "No. I think they knew that such a stunt would result in a quick death."

I intended to move the company approximately two kilometers from the ambush site. So, to confuse the enemy, we traveled in a northerly direction first in order to find a good site for calling in a medevac. Once we completed the evacuation of the two wounded VC, I set our movement on an easterly course. The plan was to move with stealth again and ambush the smaller canal during the coming night. Knowing that a trail paralleled the small canal, I issued a verbal caution to avoid exposure from the opposite canal bank for fear of an ambush.

The first 100 meters went well. I was proud of my men because I hardly heard a sound as we moved through some rough terrain. However, suddenly automatic AK fire erupted ahead of us about 50 meters, followed by a call for "medic." After hearing the urgent call, I moved in the direction of the shooting as fast as possible. Upon arrival, I learned to my chagrin that two men had wandered close to the trail and were shot by the enemy from across the canal. They both sustained serious injuries to their legs and required immediate evacuation. By the time we completed the evacuation, we had been delayed more than an hour.

As we proceeded stealthily to our next ambush site, I reminded

---

*The starlite scope was one of the first-generation scopes to absorb and modify ambient light, which enabled the user to see well at night. The starlite was designed for mounting on light infantry weapons and could be zeroed for effective fire both day and night.

Part 2—When Things Go Wrong in Combat

myself of a quote that is attributed to Sun Tzu, the great Chinese military philosopher and strategist: "Arrogant in victory—Sullen in defeat." I had experienced both emotions and knew it would not be the last time.

We completed the stealth mission with our victories outweighing our defeats. I was confident that our tactics were so out of the ordinary that we instilled great fear in the hearts and minds of the VC in that area. We delivered the two women prisoners to intelligence authorities only to learn a couple of weeks later that they were soon released. The battalion intelligence officer explained that they were wives of the VC and not involved in any military operations against us or the ARVN.

I thanked my battalion commander for granting us permission to execute the stealth mission and remain in the area for three nights and parts of four days. In the conclusion of my after-action report, I emphasized that I felt that we had made a big difference in the enemy's willingness and capability to launch attacks on the Ninth Infantry Division's base camp. I also stressed my immense pride in my soldiers.

XXIII

Left Behind

It was spring of 1969 and I had been in South Vietnam as commander of an infantry company for about four months. Because the Ninth Infantry Division base camp near the city of My Tho had been pounded several times over the past weeks with rockets and 120 mm mortars, the division commander ordered the division's infantry units to ambush major canals, roadways, and trails. In this region of South Vietnam, it was virtually impossible for the enemy to transport heavy weapons and ammunition overland. Such conditions forced the VC to rely heavily on waterways to move heavy weapons and logistical supplies. The strategy of ambushing the many waterways was effective in denying their use by the enemy, but it required constant vigilance.

My unit, which was Company C, Sixth Battalion, 31st Infantry Regiment, had been ordered into this area several times. So, many of the major waterways and trails were familiar to us. On this particular day, we were transported by medium-size trucks and dropped off in midafternoon. After we disembarked and reassembled, we made our way cautiously for a distance of about two kilometers past the small hamlets into the wooded area that was controlled most of the time by local VC guerrillas. Because the element of surprise was lost, the enemy had ample time to seed the trails, rice paddy dikes, and footbridges with booby traps. On some previous forays into this area, we had been bombarded by small mortars and threatened by automatic weapons fire and sniper fire.

It was my standing policy that we never traveled to an ambush site during daylight hours. Some sister companies of our battalion did not embrace such a policy and paid a heavy price when they were ambushed. When we traveled to within one kilometer of the ambush sites, I usually ordered a halt to our movement. As usual, I told my

Part 2—When Things Go Wrong in Combat

platoon leaders to place men about 50 meters from our flanks and to the rear for security. I ordered the third platoon to dispatch four men to secure the rear. I then told the platoon leaders to encourage their men to eat before dark, especially if they planned to heat their food.

I also seized the opportunity to rest and eat some of my C-rations, choosing to heat ham and lima beans for my main course. I opened both the can of ham and lima beans and a can of soft cheese spread. I then scooped some cheese onto my main entrée, chopped some fresh onion on top, which I acquired from a local farmer, and placed the can over a flaming heating tablet until it began to steam. I consumed the delightful medley of flavors and opened a can of fruit cocktail for dessert. After satiating my hunger, I brushed my teeth and rested beneath a nearby tree. I knew that darkness would close in soon and there would be little opportunity to rest during the night.

While sitting on the ground and leaning against the tree, I even

Captain George Mauldin resting and waiting for nightfall to move into ambush positions. An enemy sniper fired a bullet very close to his head about two minutes later. The unit sniper returned fire and killed him. March 1969.

XXIII. Left Behind

dozed for several minutes. I was jolted back to reality by the familiar serenade of crickets and other critters when they announce the transition to the night. I contacted my platoon leaders on the radio and told them that they should be prepared to move in 20 minutes. This would give them time to call in their security teams and adjust to the darkness. After receiving confirmation from the platoons that they were ready to move, I placed the first platoon on point with my command group following closely behind. The second platoon followed us, then the mortar platoon, and the third platoon brought up the rear.

Conditions forced us to walk in single file; therefore, my company of more than 90 men was strung out over more than 400 meters. We walked slowly and cautiously with frequent stops to enable the platoon on point to check for booby traps and punji pits. Crossing streams of any size was always a challenge. The bigger the stream, the more difficult it could be. Even small streams, which frequently had pole bridges in place, could be a problem—especially at night. After the first several troops crossed a narrow pole bridge with muddy boots, it became a serious hazard. It was not unusual to hear loud noises in the vicinity of such crossings, with well-worn curse words to follow as an unfortunate soldier's boots failed to grip the slippery logs.

We had been moving toward our ambush sites for about half an hour when I heard the voice of my third platoon leader on the radio.

"Charlie Six, this is Charlie Three, over."

I stopped and turned to my radio operator, who already had his arm extended—offering me the handset.

"This is Charlie Six, over."

"Roger, Charlie Six. I've got bad news. I just discovered that I left four of my men where we stopped just before dark. I posted them on security about 50 meters to our rear and really thought that they had been called in before we left that area. I need to go back to get them, over."

Stunned, I could hardly believe what my trusted platoon leader was reporting. I immediately realized that this was one of those situations that can go really bad for a unit if it is not handled properly from the outset.

"Roger. I acknowledge your message and understand fully its potential gravity."

My immediate reaction was to freeze everyone in place until the crisis at hand was resolved. Because we were so spread out, I issued the order by radio to stay put. Part of my order included the directive for all subordinate leaders to acknowledge my transmission.

I waited until I heard radio acknowledgment of my order from all platoon leaders, then I proceeded to deal with the crisis at hand.

"Charlie Three, is there a radio with these four men? Over."

"Negative, Charlie Six. They're armed with three M-16 rifles and an M-79 grenade launcher, over."

"Roger. Listen very carefully to the following instructions. You, personally, are to go back for these men. Take only your radio operator. When you are approximately 50 meters from where you left them, step off the trail and shoot a handheld flare. The flare will not only illuminate the surrounding area but will also alert these men to your presence. Then approach them slowly, calling out their names. If the flare burns out before you're reunited with them, shoot another one. You and those four men are much safer if you can see and recognize one another. And for God's sake, notify me the instant you find them and determine that they're OK, over."

"Roger. My RTO and I will be on our way as soon as he can locate a second flare, over."

"This is Charlie Six. Roger. Be careful and proceed slowly. This is an unusual and delicate situation."

Both anger and dread occupied my thoughts as I waited anxiously for words of reassurance. I could feel my heart pounding as I hoped for positive resolution to this crisis. I resisted any attempt for anger to overrule sound judgment, deciding quickly that I must remain calm and deliberate in reaching decisions and issuing instructions. Minutes seemed like hours as I waited to learn the fate of these six men. While waiting, the what-if scenarios took my thoughts to several disturbing places.

One such scenario was the possibility of the abandoned men firing on the approaching platoon leader and his RTO. Such a reaction could result in one of the lowest points in my command if I had to admit to my superior that I had left my soldiers behind in a vulnerable and confused state.

A second possibility was that the local guerrillas might have followed us and lain in wait to ambush the platoon leader and his RTO and then kill the four men who were cut off from the rest of the company.

XXIII. Left Behind

Finally, after more than 20 minutes, I heard the third platoon leader's voice on the radio.

"Charlie Six, this is Charlie Three. We've recovered the four men and everybody is safe. We're on our way back to join the rest of the company, over."

"Roger. Thanks for the update. I'm one happy and relieved man. Notify your platoon members that you're coming their way. Do you have another handheld flare?"

"Roger. I have one more flare and I'll shoot it when I'm about 50 meters from my platoon, over."

"Roger. Let me know when you've closed and you're ready to move."

As soon as the third platoon leader and his men had rejoined the company, I told the first platoon to proceed to the designated ambush sites.

As we made our way slowly and cautiously to the major canals, I thought a great deal about the recent incident. I suppressed my anger and decided to defer any discussion with my subordinates until we returned to the rear area for stand-down.

By the time the entire company reached the ambush sites and settled into positions, it was 2100 hours. For the first five hours, it appeared that it would be a dull night. However, the enemy decided to use one of the canals in the early morning hours, only to be savagely shot by one of the M-60 machine gunners of the second platoon. We made no attempt to recover the two enemy bodies or any of the equipment that they were transporting in their small boat. The large canal, whose current was very swift, was influenced by tidal action and was both deep and dangerous.

The next morning, we spent about two hours walking out of the dense woods and past the clusters of Vietnamese hooches to the major roadway where we were dropped off the previous day. We were picked up by army trucks and transported several miles to Fire Support Base Moore. Soon after arriving at the base, I called on my battalion commander, who told me that my company would remain at the firebase for two days to provide security. This respite would also enable the troops to dry their feet and treat themselves for fungus. He said that after two days at the firebase, we would conduct airmobile operations for several days.

On the afternoon of the second day at the firebase, I called the

Part 2—When Things Go Wrong in Combat

third platoon leader to the fortified bunker where my CP was set up. I read him the official letter of reprimand that I had written and told him that the letter would become a permanent part of his official personnel file. I also verbally reprimanded him, warning that should he commit any act in the future that placed his subordinates in jeopardy due to dereliction of duty, I would see to his court-martial.

After dismissing the platoon leader, I asked one of my RTOs to fetch the senior member of the foursome that was left behind. After Corporal Leitner appeared several minutes later and entered the bunker, I pointed to a chair and invited him to sit. I asked him to explain in detail what had transpired during the afternoon and evening when he and three others were placed in a position to provide rear security.

"Well, Sir, it was quite strange," he began. "Since I was the senior man, I picked a bend in the trail where I could see in both directions. Because of the potential for shooting each other, I kept the group together. After feeling comfortable that we were set up properly, we ate some rations, being careful to minimize the noise level. I didn't even think anything was unusual when darkness fell. However, I began to feel uneasy when Sergeant Spanner didn't come for us and it had been dark for more than a half hour. At that time, I moved the group a little farther from the trail and told the other three men that no one was to move until somebody came for us. I also told them that if VC guerrillas came down the trail, we were not to engage unless they initiated it. I also told them that if someone came from the direction the company had taken, no one was to utter a sound—that it could be suicidal for us to initiate contact—that we must let others make the initial contact. One of my greatest concerns, Sir, was that the Viet Cong would follow us on the trail. They had to know we were in the area. I had no doubt that we could defend ourselves from three or four VC, but a larger force might be able to overpower us. About 45 minutes after dark, we heard somebody fall from a log bridge over a small stream near us. We assumed that it was someone from the company, but we kept quiet. Soon afterward, Sergeant Spanner shot an illumination flare and began to call my name. I immediately answered him and walked out of the brush onto the trail. Sir, I've never been so glad to see another American as I was at that moment. Thank you for sending him back for us. He knew where he had left

XXIII. Left Behind

us, which made it much safer for someone to come back for us. That's about all there is to say about the incident, Sir."

I praised Corporal Leitner for his leadership and good judgment and told him that I was recommending him for the Army Commendation Medal for meritorious service. I also told him that since he was doing the work of a sergeant, he would be promoted to that rank the next day in a ceremony in front of the company.

As they say, "All's well that ends well." However, I have always maintained that I much prefer to reward and commend my subordinates for commendable actions and mature leadership.

XXIV

The Old Man's Kill

By the time this incident occurred, it was March 1969. I had been in command of a rifle company for five months and had become an old hand at anticipating the enemy's actions. I also learned some effective ways to surprise the enemy—for example, dropping off a stay-behind force of several men. More than once, the enemy foolishly pursued us and walked into our trap.

When conditions permitted, I personally shot at and hit the enemy, but such opportunities were rare. However, my actions in this story are exceptional. As commander of the unit, my CP group was not on point or even close to the leading elements of my company when we were on the move. Besides, in those instances when we engaged the enemy, there were numerous assessments and decisions that I had to make quickly. Such background tidbits are useful in appreciating why this story resonates with me. This was an exceptional incident where an unexpected responsibility fell on my shoulders. Had I not been alert, quick to shoot, and a good marksman, my senior lieutenant and his radio operator would have been shot and either severely wounded or killed.

During the day leading up to this incident, we conducted two air assault missions. At the conclusion of the second one, we loaded in a flight of 12 helicopters, which transported 72 men of my company to a designated overnight location. The choppers dropped us off and six of the choppers returned to transport the remaining 28 men. It was a thickly wooded area where we had been twice on previous operations. Our purpose in deploying to the area was to be part of the Ninth Infantry Division's security force. The area contained some high ground where the VC had dug punji pits and planted booby traps along the trails.

We cautiously entered the wood line and waited for the

XXIV. The Old Man's Kill

remainder of the men from the company. They arrived about 20 minutes later, at which time we moved farther into the woods. After organizing the company in a perimeter and ensuring that the mortars were ready for action, I encouraged the men to eat and feel free to heat their food with an open flame. It was late in the day, and I estimated that we had only 45 minutes until dark.

The company settled into the night as usual. With the exception of placing Claymore mines in front of positions, security preparations were completed before dark. After darkness closed in, an eerie quiet settled on us. I sat on the ground, leaning against a tree, reflecting on the activities of the day. I was close to my radio operators as usual. Suddenly, I heard the voice of my commander calling on the radio.

I took the handset and answered, "This is Charlie Six, over."

"This is Tango Six. There are reports from higher that probable enemy elements have been detected moving along a riverbank that is east of you. Rockets have been launched from this location recently. We'll send you the coordinates to the place of suspected enemy action immediately. Afterward, send one of your elements to that location, and let operations know when they are in place. Any questions? Over."

"This is Charlie Six. No questions. WILCO, over,"

I looked at my watch. It was 2100 hours. I told my radio operator to call all platoons and ask the platoon leaders to come to my location. As I waited for them to arrive, my radio operator on the battalion net walked over and handed me a piece of paper where he had copied the coordinates of the targeted area. I motioned for my forward observer to join me as I pulled my poncho over my head, turned on my flash light, and plotted the coordinates. It was about two kilometers from our location—across an open area that must have been 300 meters wide. A plot came to mind immediately. This was one of those rare opportunities, and I planned to take advantage of it.

When the four arrived, I motioned for them to sit in a circle around me. As I began speaking, I pointed to the third platoon leader. "Lieutenant Hauptman, I'm about to give you a delicate mission. Once we finish this meeting, you're to travel with your entire platoon due east about a kilometer. I want you to violate every discipline you've been taught. That's right! Smoke, talk, and make it appear that the entire company is moving to another location. The reason that

Part 2—When Things Go Wrong in Combat

you're relocating is because of two factors. First, we already know that the enemy launched rockets recently into the Ninth Division base camp from this general location. Second, I received hot intelligence a few minutes ago indicating that enemy elements were spotted along the riverbank where you are bound. When you arrive within a couple hundred meters of the river, proceed with caution. I don't want you to walk into an ambush. I'm giving you the scout dog. Make sure that both the dog and the handler are close to you. That dog is very good at detecting the presence of the enemy and smelling booby traps. There's a well-traveled trail that parallels the river. Ambush it and the river. The coordinates are on this paper," I stated as I leaned forward and handed over the piece of paper. I allowed a couple of minutes for him to plot the coordinates.

Afterward, I continued to explain the plot that I had in mind. "Be assured that local guerrillas are keenly aware of our presence. A full rifle company, arriving by noisy helicopters, is a big deal to them. I want to deplete their numbers if possible before we leave, and here's how. They'll not miss the movement of the third platoon when they cross the wide expanse of open ground to our east. If we can convince the guerrillas that we're no longer in this location, it's very predictable that they'll sweep this ground early tomorrow morning. So here's a big part of the master plan. After the third platoon travels to its ambush site and we've notified battalion of this fact, we'll likely receive probing fire. It's impossible to predict when it will occur, but I'm confident that it will happen. No one, I mean no one, is to return fire unless he can see the muzzle flash from the enemy's rifle. We'll have a stand-to at 0500 hours. This means that everyone is awake, alert, and ready for action. If they sweep this area as I think they will, I want to punish them. All of this movement, to include retrieving Claymores at night, is an unwelcome task. Please be careful, and make certain that everyone is aware of what's happening now and tomorrow morning. First and second platoons, shrink our perimeter accordingly and ensure that you are linked up. Any questions?"

There was a lot of noise for at least a half hour as the platoons complied with my instructions. Lieutenant Hauptman came by my CP before departing and asked if the artillery forward observer was aware of his destination and mission. I reassured him that he was fully aware of the total plan. I made a brief check of our modified perimeter and returned to my leaning tree at 2245 hours. I finally

XXIV. The Old Man's Kill

wrapped myself in my poncho liner and laid on the ground to rest, drifting off to sleep after a few minutes.

I was snatched from a dream at 0200 hours with the crack of several AK rounds. They were high and from several hundred meters to our south. I held my breath, hoping that my troops would not return fire. They did not—even after several more rounds were fired high over our position. I didn't sleep much after the probing fires. One of my radio operators nudged me at 0430 hours as I requested. I hurriedly heated some water for a cup of C-ration coffee. After gulping it down, I opened a can of C-ration peaches. I ate the peaches hurriedly and finished rounding up my gear by 0455 hours. I stood watch along with my radio operators until 0550 hours. The enemy's failure to appear as expected dashed my hopes of succeeding in thinning the ranks of the local elusive guerrillas.

At 0555 hours, I received a call from the battalion operations officer informing me of a change in plans. My company was to conduct air assault missions again, and we were to be ready for pickup in the open terrain to our east by 0700 hours. I informed all platoons to be ready to move to the pickup point by 0640 hours.

I could hear some low noises as everyone finished packing gear. The first platoon leader, Lieutenant Johnson, had set up his CP near mine, and I could hear some rustling sounds as he and his radio operator packed their gear. I bent down to pick up my pack and slip it on my back when I heard the lieutenant's radio operator whisper loudly, "There's a VC and he's got a rifle." I looked at the radio operator and determined that he was looking straight ahead and crouching. Looking to my right front, I saw a VC in uniform shouldering an AK-47 rifle and aiming it at Lieutenant Johnson and his radio operator. As fate would have it, the VC did not see me—I was not in his line of sight. I moved the selector of my M-16 from safe to fire as I shouldered it and aimed for the enemy's heart. I fired six rounds rapidly on semiautomatic and watched as the enemy soldier fell back into a cluster of shoulder-high palms. I moved to my radio operator on the company frequency and broadcast the order to all platoons to get on line from east to west for a sweep through the area. I explained what had just happened and stated that there had to be more VC fighters. I walked cautiously to the cluster of palms where the VC had fallen, expecting him to be lying on the ground. I was completely surprised to find drag marks where he had been pulled back into the woods by

Part 2—When Things Go Wrong in Combat

a comrade that I never saw. I notified my second platoon leader by radio that the drag marks went in his direction. Within 30 seconds after I spoke with the second platoon leader, I heard an M-16 being fired on automatic. The second platoon leader called on the radio and said, "One of my elements just found the VC you shot. He was drawing his last breaths, but my man shot him anyway for good measure."

I called off the sweep after about 20 minutes because we had a firm time for pickup by helicopters. We reorganized quickly and moved out to the cleared area where we were reunited with the first platoon. My first platoon leader reported that they had no action after moving to the river. I was proud of my troops and promised myself that I would compliment them as soon as we returned to the rear area.

While waiting for the choppers to arrive, I motioned for Lieutenant Johnson to join me several feet away from the others. I quickly raised the issue that was eating away at me.

"Dan, do you not realize that had I not been alert and fast with my rifle, you and your radio operator would likely be dead? Is there any credible explanation for your radio operator's behavior? He saw the VC before I did and just blurted out that the VC was standing there with a rifle."

"Yes, sir, there is. We can blame Defense Secretary McNamara for this soldier's demeanor. He's one of the 100,000, Sir, who was sent to this war zone despite their mental deficiencies. He became my radio operator because the men in the platoon couldn't trust him to behave in a normal and rational way. He cannot control his fear—he just panics and freezes. As you know, in the trenches, we must believe that the men on either side of us will fight for themselves and for us. The absence of such trust impacts troop morale in a very profound way. In order to preserve troop morale, I felt compelled to make him my radio operator. He's not as effective in that position as I would like, but it preserved morale among my fighters. The several men in this category who came to our unit have serious limitations on what they can be trusted to do. They should never have been sent to U.S. Army fighting units. By the way, Sir, thank you for saving our lives."

The lieutenant's comments made me realize the seriousness of the mental deficiencies among the last 12 replacements to report to my company. It was evident that it was a big issue deserving of an

XXIV. The Old Man's Kill

elevation in priorities. I later appealed to my superior commander to rectify this problem as soon as possible. I concluded long ago that an infantryman who could not control his fear was a danger to himself and, potentially, to others.

XXV

A Soldier Called Mouse

I arrived at the replacement center in Ben Hoa, South Vietnam in mid–October 1968, after spending the previous six months commanding an infantry unit in the famous 82d Airborne Division in North Carolina. Virtually any command time would show well on the résumé of a young officer; however, successful command of an infantry unit in a war zone would be far more impressive. Therefore, I was obsessively focused on doing everything possible to command an infantry company. My orders directed me to report to the Ninth Infantry Division, which had relocated in recent weeks to a site virtually on the banks of the Mekong River about 60 miles south of Saigon. Little did I realize that such vacancies occurred frequently in this famous division. I learned soon after arriving at the division base camp that the average longevity of a commander of an infantry company was slightly over three months—and I would soon learn why.

Within five days, I found myself in a plane loaded with replacements bound for the Ninth Infantry Division. In a single day, I accomplished the processing required at the division level which concluded with my assignment to the first brigade. I was transported by truck to the first brigade rear which was inside the Ninth Division base camp. There, I was informed that the brigade commander and his staff were deployed to a field site and that I would be transported to that location within a couple of days. While waiting, I was issued an M-16 rifle, a pack, steel helmet, 100 rounds of ammunition, two days of C-rations, and other essential gear.

In the afternoon of the second day, I loaded onto a truck that would transport another captain and me, plus 15 enlisted replacements, several miles to the first brigade CP. It was the rainy season in South Vietnam and everything was wet. Fortunately, the truck

XXV. A Soldier Called Mouse

bed was covered with canvas which protected us from the rain. I had been exposed to monsoons on my first tour; however, this was dramatically different because the scenery along the road consisted of flat ground with standing water. It was evident that flooded terrain and incessant rain would be my constant companion for the indefinite future.

Upon reaching the first brigade CP, we officers were met by a captain, who introduced himself as the brigade adjutant. He escorted us to one of two army tents, where he opened a flap and invited us to enter. Once inside, we were introduced to the brigade commander first, then some of his staff officers. A lieutenant colonel, who was standing a few feet away, stepped forward and introduced himself. He was the commander of one of the three battalions of the brigade—the Sixth Battalion, 31st Infantry. The brigade commander welcomed us and asked about our backgrounds. After several minutes, he explained our assignments, telling me that I was assigned to the Sixth Battalion, 31st Infantry. I made eye contact with the lieutenant colonel, whose name was Paterson. Having concluded that I liked him, I was thrilled to be assigned to his battalion.

When the brigade commander released us, Lieutenant Colonel Paterson motioned to me to follow him to the smaller tent nearby. After entering the tent, the senior officer invited me to sit in one of the chairs around a small, olive, drab table. When we were seated, he began to speak.

"Captain, I'm impressed with your background, and I really like the fact that you served your first tour as a lieutenant and gained a probable mountain of experience at the platoon level. I'm also pleased to see that you had a successful company-level command in the 82d Airborne Division. I'm going to give you Charlie Company. In fact, at this time, they are the security force around this forward CP. I already sent a runner to retrieve the current commander. You can accompany him to the company CP and begin the process now of transitioning. I have high expectations of you. That company had a difficult time during the Tet Offensive when the battalion was just south of Saigon. They sustained a lot of casualties. Their morale is low, and that is one of the things that I expect you to improve."

At that moment, a wet, tired, and hollow-eyed infantry captain slipped under the tent flap. I was not surprised at his appearance because I had seen it many times on my first tour. Sleepless nights,

Part 2—When Things Go Wrong in Combat

C-ration food, exhaustive treks day and night through difficult terrain, night ambushes, back-to-back air assault missions, extreme heat in the daytime, and threats of hypothermia at night take a toll over time.

I stood when the lieutenant colonel introduced me to my predecessor whose name was Captain Hannity. To this point in time, the battalion commander had not shared any details about this officer. After making small talk for a few minutes, I followed the captain through ankle-deep mud to his CP, which was set up in the ruins of a stucco-type house. His radio operators were huddled under a part of the roof that remained at one end. After meeting the several members of his CP group, I agreed to follow him around the perimeter to meet the four platoon leaders and some of the men.

As we sloshed through the mud and puddles, he began to speak. "The truck that brought you here also brought a shipment of mail. That will explain to a great degree why the men are huddled under their ponchos with their letters and packages from home. As you know, mail call is a special activity with deployed troops. Some of the smaller packages were delivered in this shipment; however, the larger packages were retained in the rear and will be delivered when the company has another stand-down for a few days."

As we made the rounds, some of the men were heating and eating food from C-ration packets. Others were lost in letters from home, yet they took their eyes from the words long enough to acknowledge me as their future commander. When we walked to the next position, we came upon two men under a poncho that was suspended over them. As we approached, I could see that one soldier began wiping tears from his cheeks upon spotting us. Captain Hannity introduced me and told them that I would be their new company commander. They both uttered pleasantries, with the short, brown man speaking with strongly accented English.

When we had distanced ourselves from the position, I asked Captain Hannity about the sad soldier. "He's an alien from Mexico and entered the army from the San Antonio, Texas, area. He's a good soldier. His name is Private Santana Torres. He's been in the U.S. a long time, but I suspect that he lived in a neighborhood where most people spoke Spanish. His English is quite poor. He's always smiling—except tonight. He must have received some sad news in the letter that he was holding. The men gave him the nickname Mouse. I

XXV. A Soldier Called Mouse

guess it's because of his pointed face and very large, shiny teeth. Of course, I never use that nickname when I speak to him."

That was the meeting in which I first came to know this man called Mouse.

One Week Later

The honeymoon period was over, with the week allotted for transition passing very quickly. I had now been on my own for a full week as the commander of this unit, which called itself "Charlie Hunter." In accordance with army tradition, I was qualified at that point to be referred to by my subordinates as "the old man." As soon as the company came to the division base camp for a two-day stand-down, I took two actions, which set the course for my time as the commander. First, I required the first sergeant to assemble the unit in a formation. I walked the ranks, faced every man and shook his hand. I said to each man, "I'm your new commander, and if you have grievances, my door is always open. We fight for each other. I've got your back, and I expect you to have mine."

The following morning, I initiated the second action when the alarm on my watch woke me at 0200 hours. I roused the first sergeant and instructed him to awaken all senior NCOs of the company and to send someone to the officers' quarters and bring all of them to the company orderly room. After they arrived, I dispatched an officer and an NCO to each barrack with instructions for one of them to stand at the front door and the other to stand at the back door. They were to rouse everyone and have each man stand by his bunk. I took the first sergeant in tow and checked every bunk, wall locker, and area around the bunk for drugs and contraband. I found a plastic bag with marijuana in it behind an exposed two-by-four-inch stud. It was behind the bunk of a man named Pittman, who denied ownership of it. I observed that Mouse occupied the bunk next to him. I searched his property, as I did all other troops, and found nothing of concern. I found more drugs and various types of contraband at other locations in my search. I was not surprised because I had been forewarned in my conversations with other officers. However, I was disappointed.

That afternoon, I asked the first sergeant to bring Mouse and his platoon leader to my office. When they arrived, I explained that my purpose was to determine why I had such a sad soldier and to look for ways to help. Mouse told me in his broken English that his father was dead and his mother was struggling financially. I told him that he was nearly due for promotion to the next rank and praised him for being a good soldier. I also promised that I would see to his promotion on time.

The Next Morning

After learning that we were destined to conduct air assault missions for the next two days, I collected all platoon leaders and platoon sergeants in my office and briefed them on the mission. I also gave them the designated time to arrive at the helicopter pickup pad. My two radio operators and I were transported in my jeep because I wanted to reach the helipad early. A few minutes later, the large army trucks began arriving with the remainder of the officers and their soldiers. Lieutenant Johnson, who was the leader of the first platoon, had assembled his men a short distance from me. I got a glimpse of Mouse, who was standing in the third rank. When our eyes met, he turned away from me quickly. I was shocked at what I saw in that instant because his right eye was dark and swollen and his bottom lip was swollen and split. He also seemed to have bruises on his face. I yelled Lieutenant Johnson's name, and when he turned in my direction, I motioned for him to come to me.

"Dan, what in the hell happened to Mouse? I spotted him in your ranks, and he looks as if he was attacked and beaten."

"I saw him earlier this morning, Sir. Yes, he was attacked by someone, but he claims that he doesn't know who beat him. Another one of my men told my platoon sergeant that Mouse was the victim of a blanket party. You know, it's when they throw a blanket over someone and he can't see who's hitting him. He also spoke of a rumor that Mouse squealed on some of the drug users when he was called into your office yesterday. It seems that some of my men suspect that he identified the owners of the drugs that you found hidden behind the two-by-four studs in the barracks. I haven't had time to get to the bottom of this issue, Sir, but I'll keep trying. Even if Mouse knows who attacked him, he may be afraid to talk."

XXV. A Soldier Called Mouse

"Damn! I never dreamed that his fellow soldiers would make such an assumption without any facts about the matter. Now I feel like hell. I guess I'm responsible to some degree. You were there when I spoke to him. So when we return from these operations, assemble your men and make damned certain that they know the truth."

Five Days Later

We were licking our wounds from a battle in one of the two air assault missions that occurred during the previous five days. We had assaulted an LZ that was occupied by a sizable enemy force. They were in bunkers with overhead cover, and they held their fire until the helicopters were within several feet of the water. To make matters worse, our targeted area was an islet in the dreaded "Plain of Reeds" where we encountered deep water that was over our heads in some places. Because we were trapped for a considerable time in deep water, the opportunistic leeches gorged themselves on our blood. The enemy force had a heavy machine gun that damaged several helicopters and actually downed one. As the damaged chopper careened out of control, all of my men, with one exception, jumped free before it plunged into the water. Pittman was unable to jump free and was trapped inside the overturned helicopter with his foot caught under its massive weight. As I learned later, Mouse heard his calls for help and tried to climb over the side of the chopper but was turned away each time by enemy fire. Then, I was told, he used the butt of his rifle to break through the windshield and swim through it underwater to help the trapped soldier. Mouse was known to be afraid of water—a factor that qualified this as a selfless and courageous act.

We ultimately prevailed in the battle, thanks to the artillery and assault helicopters. With their help, we killed 28 enemy and captured a lot of equipment, ammunition, and weapons. However, we paid a heavy price for the victory. Several of my men were wounded, and two members of the helicopter crew were killed. Mouse was very weak from the loss of blood because of the many leeches and was sick from ingesting aviation fuel. His condition required evacuation along with my radio operator and other wounded from the company.

The second day after we returned to the rear area, I visited the hospital to check on my wounded soldiers. All of the wounded men, except for Pittman and my radio operator Peters, were reported to be stabilized and ready for transfer to hospitals in Japan and the United States. I learned from the medical staff that Pittman and Peters required at least one additional surgery before they could be transferred to other locations for treatment and therapy.

When I spoke to one of the doctors about Pittman's condition, he told me that the young soldier would lose at least half of his foot. He also intimated that Pittman had been very emotional several times and on one occasion referred to being saved from drowning by the man whom he had beaten. I was stunned for a few moments. When I recovered, I told the doctor that I might know something about that statement.

In my inquiries, I found that Mouse had received several pints of blood, which stabilized him quickly. However, he was still suffering from ingesting the toxic jet fuel and was experiencing weakness from dehydration and nausea.

Three Months Later

The monsoon finally stopped by late February; however, that did not mean that we would be spared constant contact with mud and water. The majority of the delta is at or below sea level. That fact, combined with the favorable climate, enables the population of that region to grow vast amounts of rice. This fact also dictates that there are many rice growers; consequently, our movements by land required travel through these paddies. Because of the threat of booby traps, we were unable to walk on the dikes that separate the paddies and control water flow. Instead, to be safe, we were forced to walk in the rice paddies—a tiring experience that drained our energy and slowed movement.

In mid–February, I was called to the battalion TOC. While there, the commanders of the other three line companies and I were briefed on our next mission. We would assault into an area that was called "the cocked pistol" because of its shape. It was situated in the extreme southwest corner of our area of operation. We had assaulted this area in December of the previous year and found it to be well protected from ground troops with lots of booby traps. The battalion commander was prompted to conduct an assault with the entire

XXV. A Soldier Called Mouse

fighting force because intelligence assets had intercepted radio transmissions that suggested the presence of a high-level VC headquarters. If these reports were accurate, it was logical to assume that the area was well protected.

The next day, we were delivered by choppers to the north-northwest of the target. My company was inserted into a cleared area that was approximately 400 meters long by 150 meters wide. There was no enemy fire. I was under instructions to link up with Bravo Company on my left and Alpha Company on my right. A few minutes after we settled in, the operations officer notified me by radio that there was a very large fortified bunker in the middle of the thickly wooded area to my south. Furthermore, he ordered my company to assault through the wooded area to within 100 meters of the bunker. Once in position, I was to array my men linearly to prevent the enemy from escaping once the artillery began to impact.

We proceeded as directed, slowly and cautiously, always on the lookout for booby traps. We traveled at least 50 meters into the

Captain George Mauldin in a photograph that was taken by one of his radio operators while en route to the ill-fated mission in which the company encountered a minefield for the first time. Mid-February 1969.

Part 2—When Things Go Wrong in Combat

Assault helicopters in formation en route to the enemy target, which was protected by a minefield. Mid-February 1969.

wooded area before I heard the first explosion. It was accompanied by an immediate call for a medic. Within seconds, I heard the second explosion as the medic was making his way to the wounded soldiers. My command group followed the first platoon into the woods. The two injured men were from that platoon, and the platoon leader soon called me on the radio. First, he requested a medevac. Then he frantically explained that he had called a halt to movement because several of his men spotted numerous booby-trapped grenades with wires as well as antipersonnel mines. While my radio operator requested a medevac, I searched the immediate area around me. With little effort, I spotted a trip wire and the prongs of two U.S. antipersonnel mines. I felt my heart racing because I had trained on these mines and knew that they could easily maim a victim by severely injuring a foot or leg or completely severing a foot. They were detonated easily by either stepping directly on the prongs or tilting them only slightly. I was petrified and feared for my men.

I immediately called all subordinate leaders and said, "Freeze

XXV. A Soldier Called Mouse

where you are. We have a mixture of trip wire booby traps and antipersonnel mines. Without moving, I spotted several mines, and it appears that the enemy set them arbitrarily, making it difficult to detect a pattern. I'll request to withdraw from the woods. Advise your men not to move around unless it's urgent—it's too risky. I'll let you know what my superior says about my request."

My request was granted. The battalion operations officer also informed me that the other companies had suffered the same fate and were withdrawing to a safe distance from the center of the target. I breathed a sigh of relief and ordered the company to withdraw. Few threats traumatized me like mines. I heard two additional explosions as we reversed course—trying to retrace our steps. Ultimately, there were five wounded men to place on the medevac. Lieutenant Johnson also told me that Mouse had volunteered to help transport the wounded to the chopper and, in the process, was injured by a mine that was tripped by another soldier. At the time, I received a report that the blast ripped his boot but only scratched his leg.

I withdrew the company to the north side of the clearing and waited for my commander's next order. I was very relieved when the operations officer informed me that he had requested an airstrike on the target, along with 155 mm artillery. We soon heard the roar of a jet engine and saw a fighter approach, dropping several napalm and high-explosive bombs on the bunker area. There were numerous secondary explosions—signaling that some of the artillery rounds or the 500-pound bombs struck the enemy's stored munitions.

I placed my platoons in linear formation, linking up with troops from Bravo Company on one side and Alpha Company on the other. It was another sleepless night, with 155 mm artillery rounds pounding the center of the encirclement. We had brief firefights as enemy soldiers tried to sneak through our lines. In some instances, the VC attacked in strength and tried to fight their way through. Nobody gave an inch. By morning, over 100 enemy soldiers had been killed. My men had stacked over 10 enemy bodies in a pile. Many more were burned to death by the napalm or were buried alive by the artillery and the 250-pound bombs. There was no accurate count taken of the enemy dead in close proximity to the fortified bunkers. When this operation ended, Charlie Company was transported to the division base camp for a sorely needed three-day stand-down.

Part 2—When Things Go Wrong in Combat

Top and bottom: An American fighter making bombing runs on the bunker that was protected by the minefield. Mid-February 1969.

XXV. A Soldier Called Mouse

Two Days Later

Early that morning, I saw Mouse limping as he walked back from the mess hall. So when I returned to my office, I sent for Lieutenant Johnson, Sergeant Adamly, and Mouse. The young soldier was limping badly when he walked into my office. I greeted the trio and asked Mouse how he was doing. He said he was fine, but I still insisted that he remove the boot from the injured foot. I was convinced immediately that the injury was not as minor as he pretended. His right foot and ankle were swollen to twice their normal size. Additionally, there was a deep laceration in his calf muscle.

I ordered his platoon leader to ensure that Mouse was taken to the battalion aid station immediately. I further stated that if the doctor did not order at least five days of bed rest, I would. After releasing Mouse and Sergeant Adamly, I continued talking to Lieutenant Johnson. "Dan, why doesn't Mouse seek medical attention? Even with a legitimate combat injury, he says that it's not painful when we know that it must be. Can you help me understand this?"

His answer was shocking. "As I understand it, Mouse is nearly the sole financial support for his family, some of which is still in Mexico. He's all they've got, and he won't do or say anything that could jeopardize his pay. Sergeant Adamly told me that he's afraid of being labeled a malingerer if he stays in the rear area while the rest of the company is deployed on operational missions. And he's afraid that we in the chain of command might discipline him in some way that would affect his pay. I don't think that I could ever comprehend his paranoia regarding this issue."

As I matured in my assignment as commander of this collection of men, I became more immersed in operational issues, causing me to focus less on Mouse's welfare. However, the change of mission that soon followed would result in dramatic changes in how we conducted operational missions.

XXVI

A Different Mission

Near the end of March 1969, the company settled into a totally different mission. We were assigned to a small camp that the U.S. Army Corps of Engineers had constructed for the Ninth Infantry Division. It was adjacent to a small village named Vinh Kim, which was protected by a Vietnamese PF. When a company of our battalion was assigned this mission, it was required to dispatch platoon-size

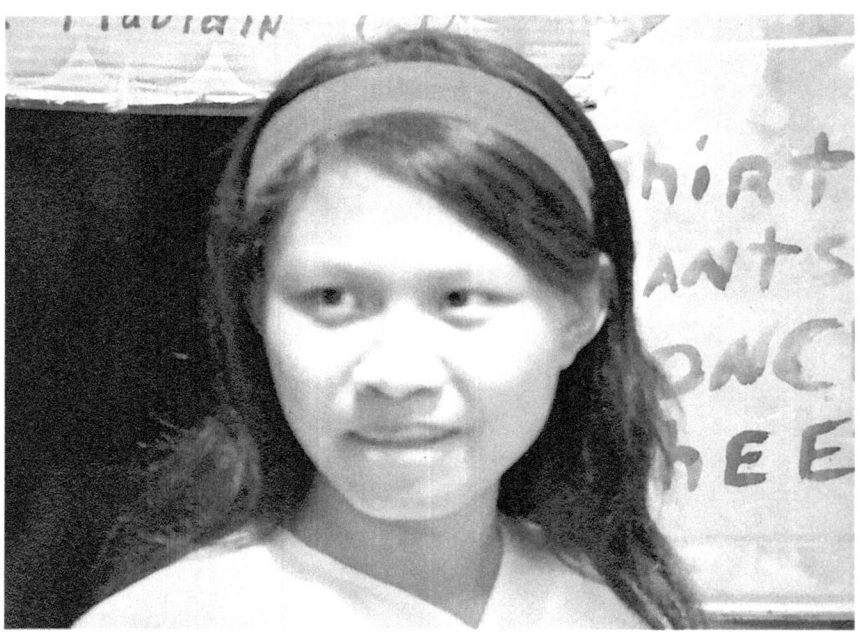

The young woman cleaned and pressed the laundry at the Vinh Kim camp. I was impressed with the quality of her work, especially given that she and several other women washed everything by hand in a local stream.

XXVI. A Different Mission

ambushes each night to the south of the camp as part of the protective force for the Ninth Infantry Division base camp.

I was unhappy with the mission at Camp Vinh Kim because I was under orders to remain in the camp while my platoons were on operational missions. The primary threats to my platoons most of the time were booby traps and an occasional sniper. One evening when I was returning from checking the security of our camp perimeter, I spotted several troops sitting in a circle. A couple of men were drinking what smelled like coffee and one was smoking a cigarette. I greeted them, and when they answered, I realized that Mouse was among them, so I asked if I could sit a spell with them. One of the men disappeared and returned with a three-legged stool. As he handed the stool to me, he said, "Engineers made several of these for us, Sir. I wouldn't lean too much in any direction with it if I was you. They fall over real easy." After settling onto the stool, I directed my attention to Mouse.

"How are your foot and leg doing, Mouse?"

"It's OK, sir. I'll be ready to go back on operations tomorrow."

"How many more days do you have in 'Nam?"

View of a section of the Vinh Kim camp perimeter. The visible weapon on top of the bunker is a recoilless rifle. March 1969.

Part 2—When Things Go Wrong in Combat

"Forty-two, sir."

"OK. What happens after 42 days? I understand that some of your family is still in Mexico, but I also know that you want to become an American citizen. So what are your plans after you get off the plane at Travis Air Force Base near San Francisco?"

"I have first to see family, Sir. I miss them, and they need me. After a few days with family, I want to go back to Texas and make papers for citizenship. My good discharge from the army makes my citizenship not so hard and slow. When I was back in the division rear area the first few days, I went to see—I think you call him JAG officer. He tell me I must apply through government office in U.S. Sir, my duty in Vietnam is mucho important to me because I need this good discharge from the army. My father, he die when my little sister was a baby, and my mother no marry another man. My mother is young woman, but she look old and tired. She work really hard, but if I no send money, they no have house and food. When I leave army, I work in California and I send money to home, and after some time, bring all my family to California."

After hearing such details from Mouse, I felt that I was finally understanding this young soldier's motives, fears, and aspirations. There was yet one issue that I felt I should explore, and this was a ripe opportunity. Did Mouse know that Pittman was his attacker when he saved him from drowning?

I rose from the stool and asked Mouse if he would move away from the group for a private conversation. Once we had moved several feet away, I turned and said, "I have to ask you a question. I realize that the subject is sensitive and personal, but I must know the answer. Was Pittman the man who beat you?"

Mouse's reaction clearly revealed that he was surprised by the question. After hesitating a few seconds, he responded, "Yes, Sir, he is the one. But please don't say anything about this to nobody else."

I moved a little closer, placed my hands on Mouse's shoulders, and said, "I was told this by the doctor who treated Pittman's injury in the hospital immediately following that big operation in the Plain of Reeds. I must say that I am overwhelmed at your courageous and selfless act to save this man from certain death in that overturned helicopter. You placed yourself in great danger to rescue him."

I remember relaxing my grip on his shoulders and stepping back a few steps. Before Mouse could respond, I asked about another issue

XXVI. A Different Mission

that was plaguing me. "How did you overcome your fear of the water so you could swim through the hole in the chopper's windshield?"

He replied, "I don't know how I do this, Sir. I hear a call for help and I try two times to go over side of chopper. When enemy see me try to climb over, he shoots many bullets at me. The next I know, I am underwater hitting on the windshield to get through."

I was in awe at the amount of courage required of him under such conditions, so I pursued the issue for confirmation. "Do you mean to tell me that you had to make the hole that you swam through?"

"Yes, sir, I beat windshield with my rifle to make hole. I go underwater three, maybe four, times to break glass. Glass very thick."

After letting his answer sink in, I said, "I hope you realize your dreams, Mouse. And if I can ever help you in any way, please let me know. I offer this help now and also after you leave the army. You're a good soldier and a good person, and you will do well wherever you go. Just hang on to your positive attitude and continue to work hard and you are bound to succeed. I'm glad that your injury is healing OK. Just take it easy so that the infected area heals thoroughly. And last but not least, be careful on operations. You have only a few more days to go in this war, and I don't want anything to happen to you."

By early April, Mouse had very few days remaining on his one-year tour, so I told Lieutenant Johnson to exclude him from overnight ambushes. In the meantime, I was very distracted by a rebellious soldier who had refused orders from me and his platoon leader to accompany his fellow soldiers on operational missions. I decided that he should be court-martialed for such an offense during wartime. Of course, I did not have such authority at the company level, so I decided to travel to the rear, process the court-martial recommendation, and forward it to the battalion commander. I returned to the division rear area by helicopter in midafternoon, and although my first sergeant and I worked feverishly to finish the paperwork, we fell short. The next day, we finished the paperwork just before noon and were in my office exploring possible ways to promote Mouse to the rank of sergeant. We were considering an available administrative measure called a "waiver of time in grade," when one of the men burst into the first sergeant's office and shouted, "First Sergeant, I was just up at the battalion aid station, and they told me that a

Part 2—When Things Go Wrong in Combat

medevac was inbound to the hospital with three wounded men from Charlie Company."

The first sergeant and I wasted no time. We jumped into my jeep and raced to the battalion TOC. Once inside, operations specialists confirmed the report that three members of the company had hit booby traps while the platoon was returning from its overnight ambush. I tried in vain to determine the names of the wounded but was told repeatedly that such detail had not yet been reported.

My first sergeant and I quickly returned to the jeep and asked the driver to drive to the evac hospital as fast as possible. We had made numerous trips to the hospital over the course of my command, so our faces were familiar to many of the medical staff and doctors. Fortunately, we commanders and senior NCOs of the line units were granted easy access to the hospital, including the emergency rooms on occasion.

As we pulled into the hospital parking area, the medevac chopper's blades were beating hard against the air, signaling that it had delivered its cargo and was off on another mission. As we walked hurriedly down the graveled walkway toward the emergency room entrance, we almost collided with the battalion chaplain.

It was not unusual to see the chaplain in the hospital, as he made rounds to visit the sick and wounded two, sometimes three, times per day. As our eyes met, he asked, "Who is it, George?" I told him that I did not know but that they were from my first platoon.

As we entered the first emergency treatment room, we saw two men on treatment tables. Medical staff members were cutting their clothes from their bodies and removing the bandages that had been applied in the field. One man, whom I recognized as one of several new replacements, was screaming hysterically, "I don't want to die. Somebody help me. I don't want to die." The second was the platoon medic, which caused me to wonder who had treated their wounds. The medic was pale and quiet. I made no attempt to engage either man in conversation at that point since medical personnel were swarming around them, asking questions, and issuing instructions to assistants as well as to the wounded soldiers. In my peripheral vision, I saw a frenzy of activity in the adjacent room. I focused my attention on that room because I still did not know the identity of the third casualty.

The chaplain met me as I made my way into the second room.

XXVI. A Different Mission

"It doesn't look good for this man, George. I'm sorry. They're doing everything possible, but it just doesn't look good."

I made my way deeper into the treatment room and literally elbowed my way to the side of the table for a better look. It was Mouse. I must have gone very pale because I felt numb. I could no longer hear the chatter from the medical staff. Just as I attained a better view, the attending doctor applied a defibrillator to Mouse's chest. I swallowed hard and winced as Mouse's body heaved from the shock. I knew that this was a resuscitative procedure, and it meant that Mouse was in serious trouble.

I never thought of myself as a religious man, but I feared God and respected people who professed to be religious. I attended religious services when possible and ensured that my men were given time to attend such services. I uttered a few prayers quietly on several occasions and gave God credit for sparing my life more than once. In that instance, however, I felt so strongly about requesting God's intervention that I fell to one knee beside Mouse's treatment

Photograph of Santana S. Fernandez, Jr., aka Mouse, taken near the unit barracks in 1969 (courtesy Gary Stoltz).

Part 2—When Things Go Wrong in Combat

table. The hand I reached up to and grasped was unresponsive and cold. It jerked rhythmically as medical personnel applied heart massage to Mouse's chest.

I prayed a prayer aloud that I can never forget—asking God to spare this young soldier. I then stood next to Mouse's treatment table until I felt someone tugging at my hand, trying to free it from Mouse's. As I looked up, I realized that it was the doctor whose words forced me to accept the reality of the situation. He said, "It's no use, Captain. He was already gone when he arrived. He never had a chance. A piece of shrapnel severed his carotid artery. Very few people survive such a wound. He lost too much blood and went into cardiac arrest before the chopper landed. I'm sorry! I'm really sorry! I can tell that you cared for this young soldier in a special way."

It took a while to regain my composure. After I did, the chaplain, my first sergeant, and I returned to the other treatment room to check on the other two casualties. A nurse told me that they were stabilized quickly and moved to Ward 3A in a different section of the hospital. Upon entering the ward, we soon spotted the two men.

First Sergeant Fuentes and the chaplain went to the bed of the new replacement. I went to the bed of the platoon medic. Before I could speak, he asked, "Did Mouse make it, Sir?" After sharing the details of Mouse's fate, I asked him to describe what happened.

"Well, sir, the new man over there spotted a red-and-white pole on the side of the trail. You know, the type we use as aiming stakes for our mortars? When he said something about the stake, Sergeant Bradley shouted out to him to leave it alone—not to touch it. Well, for reasons that only Hargrove, that new man over there, can explain, he ignored the order. He reached over and pulled it out of the ground. It must have had a trip wire for a grenade attached because it exploded almost under his feet."

"Did Mouse get hit by that grenade, too?"

"No, not right then, Sir. This new man panicked and began thrashing around, and we were all afraid he might set off another booby trap. We yelled at him to stop moving around, but he was acting crazy. It was then that Mouse went to his side, trying to calm him. You know, Mouse had an unusual ability to calm people. That's when Mouse and I got hit by the second grenade. Mouse was closer to it than I was, and a fragment cut his carotid artery. I tried to save him, Sir. I really tried!"

XXVI. A Different Mission

A couple of days later, the chaplain approached me about conducting a memorial service that included Mouse. He acknowledged that I had a special fondness for Mouse and asked if I would say a few words at the service. I agreed reluctantly—knowing that I became emotional nearly every time I thought about his untimely death and how it would surely impact his family. When it was time for the service, most of the men from my company were present, along with my battalion commander, Lieutenant Colonel Paterson.

The chaplain began the service as usual, which included singing the hymn "Amazing Grace." Following a prayer, he introduced me and said that I had agreed to say a few words about Mouse.

I remember speaking slowly and methodically. "Men, this is one of the darkest, lowest moments for me as your commander. This fellow soldier, Specialist Four Santana Torres, was an inspiration to all who knew him. He did so many good things in his relatively short life, and those of us who came to know him better are certain that he left a lot of his life's work undone. In conversations earlier today, I realized that some of you did not know his real name. We all knew him affectionately as Mouse, and he didn't mind this nickname because I asked him about it once. He was a man of small stature, but in my eyes, he was a big man. His heart must have been as big as the sky because only a man with an enormous heart could have touched so many of us as he did. He was one of the most selfless individuals I have known. To give you an example, he was severely beaten by a fellow soldier because this person mistakenly thought that Mouse had revealed information to me about drugs in the barracks. Later, Mouse risked his own life during combat operations to save this attacker from certain death. Such compassion and courage are rare. Despite being preconditioned to avoid attachments to my subordinates at all costs, Mouse earned a special place in my heart and touched my life as few others have done." As I feared, I became emotional at that point and lost my voice. Upon regaining my composure, I asked the chaplain to finish reading my remarks.

I was replaced as commander of this amazing group of Americans in late April. I had been in command of "Charlie Hunter" over six months, and when I looked in the mirror, I saw a thin, hollow-eyed infantryman staring back at me. The captain, who replaced me, was an experienced officer with a previous combat tour. His résumé gave me a good feeling about "Charlie Hunter's" new leader. I was

Part 2—When Things Go Wrong in Combat

subsequently reassigned within the battalion as the assistant operations officer. I was pleased to be in a position where I could monitor "Charlie Hunter's" activities closely, which gave me a feeling of still being attached.

In concluding this story about this amazing soldier, I feel compelled to write a few words regarding his disposition following his untimely death. He was killed on April 21, 1969, five months short of his 20th birthday. He is buried in the Fort Sam Houston National Cemetery in San Antonio, Texas. I visited his grave in 2015 in the company of another veteran who had become acquainted with Mouse in Vietnam.

I purchased a brick with his name and unit etched on it, which is placed in the "Walk of Honor" at the National Infantry Museum in Columbus, Georgia. The purchase of that brick not only helps to fund the museum but also serves to ensure that Sergeant Santana S. Fernandez, Jr., is never forgotten.

Military History: Colonel (Ret.) George R. Mauldin

- 1960: enlisted in U.S. Army
- March 1960–August 1960: trained as artillery crewman and surveyor, **Fort Sill, OK**
- October 1960–April 1963: 14th Field Artillery in **Furth, Germany** (promoted to sergeant)
- June 1963–August 1964: 197th Infantry Brigade, **Fort Benning, GA**. Served as intelligence specialist and surveyor
- August 1964–February 1965 Infantry Officer Candidate School, **Fort Benning, GA**
- February 15, 1965: Commissioned as second lieutenant in infantry branch
- February 1965–May 1965: Airborne Training and Battalion Mortar and Davy Crocket (nuclear weapon) Course, **Ft. Benning, GA**
- May 1965–December 1965: Second Battalion, 41st Infantry (Mechanized), **Fort Hood, TX**
- January 1966–December 1966: mortar platoon leader and company executive officer, Company D, Second Battalion, Eighth Cavalry, First Cavalry Division (Airmobile), **An Khe, South Vietnam**
- January 1967–February 1968: Weapons Department, U.S. Army Infantry School, **Ft. Benning, GA**. Served as chief, mortar committee. Promoted to captain
- February 1968–September 1968: Commander, 55th Infantry Platoon (Davy Crocket), 82d Division Artillery, 82d Airborne, Division, **Ft. Bragg, NC**
- October 1968–April 1969: commander, Company C, Sixth

Military History: Colonel (Ret.) George R. Mauldin

Battalion, 31st Infantry, Ninth Infantry Division, **Mekong Delta, South Vietnam**

- May 1969–July 1969: assistant operations officer, Sixth Battalion, 31st Infantry. Also served in First Brigade as assistant operations officer for air operations, **South Vietnam**
- July 5, 1969–October 15, 1969: acting operations officer, First Brigade, Ninth Infantry Division, Schofield Barracks, **Oahu, HI**
- January 5, 1970–August 15, 1970: student, Infantry Officer's Advance Course, **Ft. Benning, GA**
- August 1970–August 1972: degree completion at University of Tampa, **Tampa, FL**, business major with minor in economics
- September 1972–August 1973: Arabic-language training, **Presidio of Monterey, CA**, Language Institute
- October 1973–July 1975: U.S. military training mission to **Saudi Arabia**. Promoted to major
- August 1975–June 1976: U.S. Army Command and General Staff College, **Ft. Leavenworth, KS**
- July 1976–June 1977: **University of Utah**, MA in Middle East studies with concentration in the Arabic language
- June 1977–August 1979: Defense Intelligence Agency, **Arlington, VA**—all source intelligence analyst—Iraqi ground forces
- August 1979–June 1980: attaché training and Hebrew training, **Rosslyn, VA**. Promoted to lieutenant colonel
- June 1980–July 1983: military attaché, **Tel Aviv, Israel**
- August 1983–August 1985: commander, Eighth Psychological Operations Battalion, Fourth Psyop Group, First Special Operations Command, **Ft. Bragg, NC**
- September 1985–August 1987: chief, Political/Military Division, J-5 Directorate, U.S. Central Command, **MacDill AFB, Tampa, FL**. Promoted to colonel
- Two special assignments: (1) July 1986 special assessment mission to **Djibouti and Somalia**; (2) August–October 1986 chief, Forward Headquarters Element, U.S. Central Command in **Manama, Bahrain**
- August 1987–August 1988: selected for attendance at U.S Army War College; instead, spent year at Harvard University Center for Middle East Studies as visiting Middle East scholar, **Boston, MA**
- September 1988–June 1989: assigned to Pentagon in Directorate for Logistics (Foreign Military Sales), **Washington, D.C.**

Military History: Colonel (Ret.) George R. Mauldin

- July 1989–July 1991: chief, Office of Military Cooperation, U.S. embassy, **Muscat, Sultanate of Oman**. Present for full duration of Operation Desert Shield and Operation Desert Storm
- August 1991–February: 1992 U.S. Army War College, **Carlisle, PA**, chief, Middle East Studies
- February 1992: retired from active duty

Index

AH-1 Cobra Attack Helicopter 119–120
Air Cushion Vehicle (ACV) 49, 119
Air Mobile Operations 41; air assault 77, 126
AK-47 rifle 62
An Khe 28–29, 36, 70
anti-personnel mines 170–171
Army Commendation Medal 155
ARVN 51, 104, 148

Bach Army Community Hospital, Fort Campbell, Kentucky 22
Bong Son 23, 57, 64, 70
booby trap 45, 74–75, 85, 88, 126–127, 135, 137, 142–143, 151, 156, 158, 168–171, 175, 180
Buddha 47

C-ration 19, 22, 27, 33, 41, 64
C-4 explosive 44
C-130 Aircraft 29
California 129
Camp Vinh Kim 175
Caribou Aircraft 35
Central Highlands 2, 5, 11, 16, 23, 36, 51, 64, 74, 139
Chieu hoi 45, 58, 94
Chinese 126–127
Claxton Fruit Cake 37, 39
Claymore Mine 157–158
Communist 43
CP (Command Post) 23, 27, 64, 96, 121–122, 131, 138, 145, 156, 159, 162, 164

dai wee (Vietnamese for captain) 50

82d Airborne Division 37
English (language) 50
Europeans 82

.50 caliber machine gun 65
Fire Support Base Moore 108, 117, 136, 153
1st Cavalry Division (Airmobile) 15–16, 64, 70
Fort Benning, Georgia 111
French 132, 138

Gabriel 37
Guam 28
Guatamala 43

Hanoi 58
Harassment and Incendiary Fires (H&I) 20
Hebrew 1
hooch 21, 41, 43–44, 50–52, 57–58, 77, 86–83, 92, 96, 105, 111, 121–133, 133, 137–139, 141–145, 153

Israel 1

Japan 129, 168
judge advocate general (JAG) 81

Katyusha Rocket 65
Kontum 36, 64
Korean War 109

leeches 24, 167
LOCH (light observation helicopter) 119–120, 122–123
LZ (landing zone) 16, 23, 46, 70, 72, 74, 87, 99, 128, 131, 167; LZ English 27–28, 37–38

M-79 Grenadiers 87
malaria 19
McNamara, Robert (Defense Secretary) 160

187

Index

medevac 47, 60, 71–73, 76, 78, 84–85, 87, 98–99, 101, 103–105, 112, 121, 127, 129, 134, 142, 146–147
Mekong Delta 2, 5, 45, 86, 96, 100, 110, 136, 140
Mekong River 49, 82, 93, 119–120, 162
Mexico 164, 173, 176
MPC (military payment certificate) 36–38

NCOC (Non-Commissioned Officer's Course) 111
9th Infantry Division 41, 49, 130, 136–137, 148–149, 156, 162, 174–175
NVA (North Vietnam Army) 11, 16, 27, 32, 46, 57, 60–61, 63, 69, 77

OCS (Officer Candidate School) 1
Oman 1
106mm recoilless rifle 65
orangutans 67

Pacific Ocean 82
Paris 1
Plain of Reeds 176
Pleiku 16, 36, 64
Pleime 64
point-man 11
POW (prisoner of war) 95, 99, 112–115, 117–118, 145
PRC Radio 62
Punji 11, 151, 156

Qui Nhon 29, 33

RF/PF (Regional Forces/Popular Forces) 100–101, 104–105, 170, 174
Riverine Force 93
RPG (rocket propelled grenade) 65, 130

Saigon 50, 52, 86, 110, 130, 162, 163
Sampan 51, 53, 84, 94–97, 120, 124, 145–147
San Antonio 164
San Francisco 174
Saudi Arabia 1
scout dog 158
SITREP 141–142
South China Sea 27, 39, 96, 120
South Vietnam 16, 23, 26, 43, 45, 47, 49, 64, 74, 82, 100, 149, 162
spider hole 60

Tet Offensive 163
Tiger Scout 43, 112, 122, 142
TOC (Tactical Operations Center) 57–59, 130, 136–137, 168
Travis Air Force Base 176

UH-1 Huey Helicopter 16–17, 69
United States 16, 40, 58–59. 60–61, 168
U.S. Army 117, 160
U.S Army Corps of Engineers 174
U.S. Navy boats 32

Viet Cong 5, 51, 66, 90, 111, 123; VC 11, 27, 41, 43, 52, 67, 82, 86–88, 90–91, 95, 101, 103, 105, 107, 111–113, 120, 122, 124, 130–131, 136–138, 141–143, 145, 146–149, 154, 156, 159, 169, 171
Viet Minh 82
Vietnam 36, 42, 46–47, 58–59, 85, 92, 104, 128, 176
Vietnam War 1

WILCO 157
World War II 49, 119

www.ingramcontent.com/pod-product-compliance
Lightning Source LLC
Chambersburg PA
CBHW021858230426
43671CB00006B/432